Ninja Foodi Smart Dual Zone Air Fryer Cookbook for Beginners

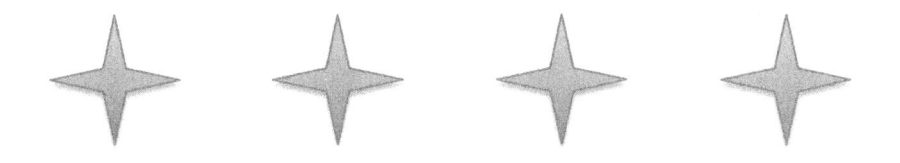

1600 Days of Easy, Delicious & Foolproof Recipes to Fry, Roast, Grill & Bake—Double the Flavor, Half the Effort

Tammy E. Lopez

All Rights Reserved.

The contents of this book may not be reproduced, copied or transmitted without the direct written permission of the author or publisher. Under no circumstances will the publisher or the author be held responsible or liable for any damage, compensation or pecuniary loss arising directly or indirectly from the information contained in this book.

Legal notice. This book is protected by copyright. It is intended for personal use only. You may not modify, distribute, sell, use, quote or paraphrase any part or content of this book without the consent of the author or publisher.

Notice Of Disclaimer.

Please note that the information in this document is intended for educational and entertainment purposes only. Every effort has been made to provide accurate, up-to-date, reliable and complete information. No warranty of any kind is declared or implied. The reader acknowledges that the author does not engage in the provision of legal, financial, medical or professional advice. The content in this book has been obtained from a variety of sources. Please consult a licensed professional before attempting any of the techniques described in this book. By reading this document, the reader agrees that in no event shall the author be liable for any direct or indirect damages, including but not limited to errors, omissions or inaccuracies, resulting from the use of the information in this document.

CONTENTS

INTRODUCTION 8

Bread And Breakfast 9

    Thai Turkey Sausage Patties 9

    Cream Cheese Deviled Eggs 10

    Pigs In A Blanket 11

    Colorful French Toast Sticks 13

    Light Frittata 14

    Chia Seed Banana Bread 15

    All-in-one Breakfast Toast 16

    Cheddar & Egg Scramble 17

    Fluffy Vegetable Strata 18

Appetizers And Snacks 19

    Spiced Roasted Pepitas 19

    Blistered Shishito Peppers 20

    Fried Pickles 21

    Roasted Jalapeño Salsa Verde 22

    Corn Dog Muffins 23

    Beer Battered Onion Rings 24

    Artichoke-spinach Dip 25

    Rumaki 26

Spicy Pearl Onion Dip 27

Hot Cauliflower Bites 28

Poultry Recipes 29

Maple Bacon Wrapped Chicken Breasts 29

Fennel & Chicken Ratatouille 30

Sunday Chicken Skewers 32

Tandoori Chicken Legs 33

Smoky Chicken Fajita Bowl 34

Satay Chicken Skewers 35

Chicken Burgers With Blue Cheese Sauce 36

Cheesy Chicken-avocado Paninis 37

Chicken Parmigiana 38

Thai Chicken Drumsticks 39

Beef, Pork & Lamb Recipes 41

Blossom Bbq Pork Chops 41

Leftover Roast Beef Risotto 42

Rib Eye Cheesesteaks With Fried Onions 43

Steak Fajitas 44

Venison Backstrap 45

Carne Asada 46

Beef & Spinach Sautée 47

Smokehouse-style Beef Ribs 48

Classic Salisbury Steak Burgers 49

Sirloin Steak Bites With Gravy 51

Fish And Seafood Recipes 52

Classic Crab Cakes 52

Spiced Shrimp Empanadas 53

Crabmeat-stuffed Flounder 54

Corn & Shrimp Boil 56

Mediterranean Salmon Cakes 57

Feta & Shrimp Pita 58

British Fish & Chips 59

Korean-style Fried Calamari 60

Creole Tilapia With Garlic Mayo 61

Speedy Shrimp Paella 62

Vegetarian Recipes 63

Spicy Sesame Tempeh Slaw With Peanut Dressing 63

Veggie Fried Rice 65

Two-cheese Grilled Sandwiches 66

Tandoori Paneer Naan Pizza 67

Roasted Veggie Bowls 68

Veggie Burgers 69

Pesto Pepperoni Pizza Bread 70

Rigatoni With Roasted Onions, Fennel, Spinach And Lemon Pepper Ricotta 71

Meatless Kimchi Bowls 72

Caprese-style Sandwiches 73

Vegetable Side Dishes Recipes 75

Toasted Choco-nuts 75

Simple Baked Potatoes With Dill Yogurt 76

Citrusy Brussels Sprouts 77

Five-spice Roasted Sweet Potatoes 77

Patatas Bravas 78

Onion Rings 79

Tasty Brussels Sprouts With Guanciale 80

Steak Fries 81

Buttered Brussels Sprouts 82

Green Peas With Mint 83

Sandwiches And Burgers Recipes 84

Dijon Thyme Burgers 84

Provolone Stuffed Meatballs 86

Chicken Gyros 87

Perfect Burgers 89

Chili Cheese Dogs 90

Black Bean Veggie Burgers 91

Reuben Sandwiches 93

Eggplant Parmesan Subs 94

Inside Out Cheeseburgers 95

Asian Glazed Meatballs 96

Desserts And Sweets 98

Strawberry Donuts 98

Strawberry Pastry Rolls 99

Oatmeal Blackberry Crisp 100

Strawberry Donut Bites 101

Hasselback Apple Crisp 102

Dark Chocolate Peanut Butter S'mores 104

Pecan-oat Filled Apples 105

Peanut Butter-banana Roll-ups 105

Black And Blue Clafoutis 106

Vegan Brownie Bites 108

INDEX 109

INTRODUCTION

Tired of bland meals, wasted time in the kitchen, and recipes that never quite turn out right?
You're not alone. Most home cooks struggle to balance flavour, health, and convenience—and that's exactly why this book exists.

The Ninja Foodi Smart Dual Zone Air Fryer is a game-changer. It lets you fry, roast, grill, and bake with less oil, less mess, and less effort. Best of all, the Dual Zone technology means you can cook two dishes at once—crispy chips in one drawer and juicy chicken in the other—ready at the same time.

This cookbook is your shortcut to making the most of it. Inside, you'll find:
✔ 1600 days of tried-and-tested recipes anyone can follow
✔ Step-by-step instructions designed for beginners
✔ British favourites made healthier—from roast lamb to fish and chips
✔ Family-friendly, budget-friendly meals that work for busy households
✔ Inspiration for every craving—snacks, mains, sides, even desserts

Cooking at home doesn't have to be stressful. With this guide, you'll discover how to turn everyday **ingredient**s into crispy, juicy, flavour-packed meals with minimal effort.

If you want to eat better, save time, and enjoy cooking again, this book is your perfect starting point.

Your journey to smarter, healthier, and more delicious cooking starts now.

Bread And Breakfast

Thai Turkey Sausage Patties

Servings: 4
Prep Time: 10 Minutes | Cooking Time: 30 Minutes
Ingredients:
- 340g turkey sausage
- 1 tsp onion powder
- 1 tsp dried coriander
- ¼ tsp Thai curry paste
- ¼ tsp red pepper flakes
- Salt and pepper to taste

Directions:
1. Preheat air fryer to 175°C/350°F.
2. Place the sausage, onion powder, coriander, curry paste, red pepper flakes, salt, and black pepper in a large bowl and mix well.
3. Form into eight patties.
4. Arrange the patties on the greased air fryer basket and air fry for 10 minutes, flipping once halfway through.
5. Once cooked, transfer patties to a plate and serve hot.
6. **Variations & Ingredients Tips:**
7. Use ground turkey or chicken instead of sausage.
8. Add grated ginger or lemongrass for more Thai flavor.
9. Serve with a sweet chili sauce for dipping.
10. **Per serving:** Calories: 195; Total Fat: 12g; Saturated Fat: 3g; Cholesterol: 70mg; Sodium: 540mg; Total Carbs: 2g; Dietary Fiber: 1g; Total Sugars: 0g; Protein: 20g

Cream Cheese Deviled Eggs

Servings: 4
Prep Time: 10 Minutes | Cooking Time: 20 Minutes
Ingredients:
- 2 cooked bacon slices, crumbled
- 4 whole eggs
- 2 tablespoons mayonnaise
- 1 teaspoon yellow mustard
- ½ teaspoon dill pickle juice
- 1 teaspoon diced sweet pickles
- Salt and pepper to taste
- 2 tablespoons cream cheese
- Parsley for sprinkling

Directions:
1. Preheat air fryer at 120°C/250°F. Place egg in the frying basket and Air Fry for 15 minutes. Then place them immediately into a bowl with ice and 240 ml of water to stop the cooking process. Let chill for 5 minutes, then carefully peel them.
2. Cut egg in half lengthwise and spoon yolks into a bowl. Arrange the egg white halves on a plate.
3. Mash egg yolks with a fork. Stir in mayonnaise, mustard, pickle juice, diced pickles, salt, pepper and cream cheese.
4. Pour 1 tablespoon of the mixture into egg white halves, scatter with crumbled bacon and parsley and serve.
5. **Variations & Ingredients Tips:**
6. Use different types of pickles, such as bread and butter or spicy, for a variety of flavors.
7. Add some smoked paprika or cayenne pepper to the yolk mixture for a smoky and spicy kick.
8. For a healthier version, replace half of the mayonnaise with Greek yogurt.
9. **Per Serving:** Calories: 190; Total Fat: 16g; Saturated Fat: 5g; Cholesterol: 195mg; Sodium: 320mg; Total Carbs: 2g; Fiber: 0g; Sugars: 1g; Protein: 9g

Pigs In A Blanket

Servings: 10
Prep Time: 10 Minutes | Cooking Time: 8 Minutes
Ingredients:
- 1 cup all-purpose flour, plus more for rolling
- 1 tsp baking powder
- 1/4 cup salted butter, cut into pieces
- 1/2 cup buttermilk
- 10 fully cooked breakfast sausage links
- Egg wash (1 egg whisked with 2 tbsp water)
- Cooking spray

Directions:
1. In a bowl, whisk flour and baking powder. Cut in butter until crumbly.
2. Make a well, pour in buttermilk and mix into a dough.
3. On a floured surface, roll out dough to 1.3-cm thick.
4. Cut 10 rounds using a biscuit cutter.
5. Place a sausage link at the edge of each round and roll up, sealing edges.
6. Brush biscuits with egg wash and spray with cooking oil.
7. Place in air fryer basket spaced apart. Air fry at 170°C/340°F for 8 mins.
8. **Variations & Ingredients Tips:**
9. Use puff pastry or crescent roll dough instead of biscuit dough.
10. Add grated cheese or chopped herbs to the dough.
11. Serve with mustard, maple syrup or hot sauce for dipping.
12. **Per serving:** Calories: 180; Total Fat: 10g; Saturated Fat: 4g; Cholesterol: 20mg; Sodium: 400mg; Total Carbs: 17g; Dietary Fiber: 1g; Sugars: 1g; Protein: 5g

Banana-blackberry Muffins

Servings: 6
Prep Time: 10 Minutes | Cooking Time: 20 Minutes

Ingredients:
- 1 ripe banana, mashed
- ½ cup milk
- 1 tsp apple cider vinegar
- 1 tsp vanilla extract
- 2 tbsp ground flaxseed
- 2 tbsp coconut sugar
- ¾ cup all-purpose flour
- 1 tsp baking powder
- ½ tsp baking soda
- ¾ cup blackberries

Directions:
1. Preheat air fryer to 177°C/350°F.
2. Place banana in a bowl and stir in milk, vinegar, vanilla, flaxseed and coconut sugar.
3. In another bowl, combine flour, baking powder and baking soda.
4. Pour dry **ingredient**s into banana mixture and stir gently to combine.
5. Divide batter between 6 muffin molds and top each with blackberries, pressing slightly.
6. Bake 16 minutes until golden brown and a toothpick comes out clean.
7. Allow to cool before serving.
8. **Variations & Ingredients Tips:**
9. Use raspberries or blueberries instead of blackberries.
10. Add chopped nuts or crystallized ginger to the batter.
11. Substitute oat or almond milk for regular milk.
12. **Per Serving:** Calories: 125; Total Fat: 2g; Saturated Fat: 0g; Cholesterol: 0mg; Sodium: 170mg; Total Carbs: 25g; Dietary Fiber: 3g; Total Sugars: 9g; Protein: 3g

Colorful French Toast Sticks

Servings: 4
Prep Time: 10 Minutes | Cooking Time: 20 Minutes
Ingredients:
- 1 egg
- ⅓ cup whole milk
- Salt to taste
- ½ teaspoon ground cinnamon
- ½ teaspoon ground chia seeds
- 1 cup crushed pebbles
- 4 sandwich bread slices, each cut into 4 sticks
- ¼ cup honey

Directions:
1. Preheat air fryer at 190°C/375°F.
2. Whisk the egg, milk, salt, cinnamon and chia seeds in a bowl. In another bowl, add crushed cereal.
3. Dip breadsticks in the egg mixture, then dredge them in the cereal crumbs.
4. Place breadsticks in the greased frying basket and Air Fry for 5 minutes, flipping once.
5. Serve with honey as a dip.
6. **Variations & Ingredients Tips:**
7. Use different types of bread, such as whole wheat or brioche, for a variety of flavors and textures.
8. Add some vanilla extract or orange zest to the egg mixture for extra flavor.
9. For a savory version, replace the cinnamon and honey with garlic powder and marinara sauce for dipping.
10. **Per Serving:** Calories: 240; Total Fat: 5g; Saturated Fat: 1.5g; Cholesterol: 50mg; Sodium: 330mg; Total Carbs: 43g; Fiber: 2g; Sugars: 18g; Protein: 7g

Light Frittata

Servings: 4
Prep Time: 10 Minutes | Cooking Time: 25 Minutes
Ingredients:
- ½ red bell pepper, chopped
- 1 shallot, chopped
- 1 baby carrot, chopped
- 1 tablespoon olive oil
- 8 egg whites
- 79 ml milk
- 2 teaspoons grated Parmesan cheese

Directions:
1. Preheat air fryer to 175°C/350°F. Toss the red bell pepper, shallot, carrot, and olive oil in a baking pan. Put in the fryer and Bake for 4-6 minutes until the veggies are soft. Shake the basket once during cooking. Whisk the egg whites in a bowl until fluffy and stir in milk. Pour the mixture over the veggies. Toss some Parmesan cheese on top and put the pan back into the fryer. Bake for 4-6 minutes or until the frittata puffs. Serve and enjoy!
2. **Variations & Ingredients Tips:**
3. Add some chopped spinach, kale or arugula for extra greens.
4. Sprinkle with crumbled feta, goat cheese or shredded mozzarella.
5. Top with sliced avocado, salsa or hot sauce before serving.
6. **Per Serving:** Calories: 86; Total Fat: 5g; Saturated Fat: 1g; Cholesterol: 3mg; Sodium: 106mg; Total Carbs: 3g; Dietary Fiber: 1g; Total Sugars: 2g; Protein: 8g

Chia Seed Banana Bread

Servings: 6
Prep Time: 10 Minutes | Cooking Time: 35 Minutes

Ingredients:
- 2 bananas, mashed
- 2 tbsp sunflower oil
- 2 tbsp maple syrup
- ½ tsp vanilla extract
- ½ tbsp chia seeds
- ½ tbsp ground flaxseeds
- 1 cup pastry flour
- ¼ cup sugar
- ½ tsp ground cinnamon
- 1 orange, zested
- ¼ tsp salt
- ¼ tsp ground nutmeg
- ½ tsp baking powder

Directions:
1. Preheat air fryer to 177°C/350°F.
2. In a bowl, mix bananas, oil, syrup, vanilla, chia and flax seeds.
3. Add flour, sugar, cinnamon, orange zest, salt, nutmeg and baking powder. Stir to combine.
4. Pour batter into a greased baking pan and smooth top.
5. Bake for 25 minutes until a knife inserted in center comes out clean.
6. Remove, let cool briefly, then cut into wedges.
7. Serve warm.
8. **Variations & Ingredients Tips:**
9. Add chopped nuts or chocolate chips to the batter.
10. Substitute whole wheat pastry flour for all-purpose.
11. Top with streusel topping before baking.
12. **Per Serving:** Calories: 205; Total Fat: 6g; Saturated Fat: 0.5g; Cholesterol: 0mg; Sodium: 170mg; Total Carbs: 36g; Dietary Fiber: 4g; Total Sugars: 15g; Protein: 3g

All-in-one Breakfast Toast

Servings: 1
Prep Time: 5 Minutes | Cooking Time: 10 Minutes
Ingredients:
- 1 strip bacon, diced
- 1 slice 2.5cm thick bread
- 1 tablespoon softened butter (optional)
- 1 egg
- Salt and freshly ground black pepper
- ¼ cup grated Colby or Jack cheese

Directions:
1. Preheat air fryer to 205°C/400°F.
2. Air fry the bacon for 3 minutes, shaking basket occasionally. Remove bacon to a plate.
3. Use a paring knife to cut a circle halfway through the bread slice, creating an indentation. Spread butter in indentation if desired.
4. Transfer bread to air fryer basket, indentation side up. Crack egg into indentation and season with salt and pepper.
5. Air fry at 193°C/380°F for 5 minutes. Sprinkle cheese and bacon around egg yolk.
6. Air fry 1-2 more minutes until cheese melts and egg is cooked to desired doneness. Serve immediately.
7. **Variations & Ingredients Tips:**
8. Use different cheese varieties like cheddar or Swiss
9. Add veggies like spinach, tomatoes or avocado
10. Cook the bacon fully before adding to get it extra crispy
11. **Per Serving:** Calories: 430; Total Fat: 27g; Saturated Fat: 12g; Cholesterol: 240mg; Sodium: 630mg; Total Carbs: 27g; Dietary Fiber: 1g; Total Sugars: 4g; Protein: 20g

Cheddar & Egg Scramble

Servings: 4
Prep Time: 5 Minutes | Cooking Time: 20 Minutes

Ingredients:
- 8 eggs
- ¼ cup buttermilk
- ¼ cup milk
- Salt and pepper to taste
- 3 tbsp butter, melted
- 1 cup grated cheddar
- 1 tbsp minced parsley

Directions:
1. Preheat air fryer to 177°C/350°F.
2. Whisk eggs, buttermilk, milk, salt and pepper until foamy. Set aside.
3. Put melted butter in a cake pan and pour in egg mixture.
4. Air fry for 7 minutes, stirring occasionally.
5. Stir in cheddar and cook 2-4 more minutes until eggs are set.
6. Remove and transfer to a plate.
7. Garnish with minced parsley.
8. **Variations & Ingredients Tips:**
9. Add cooked bacon, ham or veggies to the scramble.
10. Use different cheese like pepper jack or goat.
11. Serve with toast, breakfast potatoes or fruit on the side.
12. **Per Serving:** Calories: 270; Total Fat: 20g; Saturated Fat: 9g; Cholesterol: 340mg; Sodium: 390mg; Total Carbs: 5g; Dietary Fiber: 0g; Total Sugars: 4g; Protein: 17g

Fluffy Vegetable Strata

Servings: 4
Prep Time: 15 Minutes | Cooking Time: 30 Minutes
Ingredients:
- ½ red onion, thickly sliced
- 8 asparagus, sliced
- 1 baby carrot, shredded
- 227 g mushrooms, sliced
- ½ red bell pepper, chopped
- 2 bread slices, cubed
- 3 eggs
- 3 tablespoons milk
- 113 g mozzarella cheese
- 2 teaspoons chives, chopped

Directions:
1. Preheat air fryer to 165°C/330°F. Add the red onion, asparagus, carrots, mushrooms, red bell pepper, mushrooms, and 15 ml of water to a baking pan. Put it in the air fryer and Bake for 3-5 minutes, until crispy. Remove the pan, add the bread cubes, and shake to mix. Combine the eggs, milk, and chives and pour them over the veggies. Cover with mozzarella cheese. Bake for 12-15 minutes. The strata should puff up and set, while the top should be brown. Serve hot.
2. **Variations & Ingredients Tips:**
3. Use different veggies like spinach, zucchini, tomatoes or broccoli based on preference.
4. Swap mozzarella for cheddar, Swiss or feta cheese.
5. Add some cooked sausage, bacon or ham for a meaty version.
6. **Per Serving:** Calories: 232; Total Fat: 12g; Saturated Fat: 6g; Cholesterol: 161mg; Sodium: 314mg; Total Carbs: 16g; Dietary Fiber: 2g; Total Sugars: 5g; Protein: 16g

Appetizers And Snacks

Spiced Roasted Pepitas

Servings: 4
Prep Time: 5 Minutes | Cooking Time: 25 Minutes
Ingredients:
- 2 cups pumpkin seeds
- 1 tbsp butter, melted
- Salt and pepper to taste
- ½ tsp shallot powder
- ½ tsp smoked paprika
- ½ tsp dried parsley
- ½ tsp garlic powder
- ¼ tsp dried chives
- ¼ tsp dry mustard
- ¼ tsp celery seed

Directions:
1. Preheat air fryer to 165°C/325°F. Combine the pumpkin seeds, butter, and salt in a bowl. Place the seed mixture in the frying basket and roast for 13 minutes, turning once. Transfer to a medium serving bowl. Stir in shallot powder, paprika, parsley, garlic powder, chives, dry mustard, celery seed, and black pepper. Serve right away.
2. **Variations & Ingredients Tips:**
3. Add a pinch of cayenne pepper or red pepper flakes for a spicy kick.
4. Experiment with different herbs and spices like cumin, curry powder, or rosemary.
5. Enjoy as a snack or use as a crunchy topping for salads, soups, or roasted vegetables.
6. **Per Serving:** Calories: 320; Total Fat: 26g; Saturated Fat: 5g; Sodium: 150mg; Total Carbohydrates: 11g; Dietary Fiber: 4g; Total Sugars: 0g; Protein: 15g

Blistered Shishito Peppers

Servings: 3
Prep Time: 5 Minutes | Cooking Time: 5 Minutes

Ingredients:
- 170 g Shishito peppers
- Vegetable oil spray
- For garnishing Coarse sea or kosher salt and lemon wedges

Directions:
1. Preheat the air fryer to 200°C/400°F.
2. Put the peppers in a bowl and lightly coat them with vegetable oil spray. Toss gently, spray again, and toss until the peppers are glistening but not drenched.
3. Pour the peppers into the basket, spread them into as close to one layer as you can, and air-fry for 5 minutes, tossing and rearranging the peppers at the 2- and 4-minute marks, until the peppers are blistered and even blackened in spots.
4. Pour the peppers into a bowl, add salt to taste, and toss gently. Serve the peppers with lemon wedges to squeeze over them.
5. **Variations & Ingredients Tips:**
6. Use Padrón peppers instead of shishitos.
7. Sprinkle with togarashi or furikake seasoning for an Asian twist.
8. Serve with a soy-ginger dipping sauce.
9. **Per serving:** Calories: 25; Total Fat: 1g; Saturated Fat: 0g; Cholesterol: 0mg; Sodium: 153mg; Total Carbs: 4g; Dietary Fiber: 1g; Total Sugars: 2g; Protein: 1g

Fried Pickles

Servings: 2
Prep Time: 10 Minutes | Cooking Time: 15 Minutes

Ingredients:
- 1 egg
- 1 tablespoon milk
- ¼ teaspoon hot sauce
- 2 cups sliced dill pickles, well drained
- ¾ cup breadcrumbs
- oil for misting or cooking spray

Directions:
1. Preheat air fryer to 200°C/390°F.
2. Beat together egg, milk, and hot sauce in a bowl large enough to hold all the pickles.
3. Add pickles to the egg wash and stir well to coat.
4. Place breadcrumbs in a large plastic bag or container with lid.
5. Drain egg wash from pickles and place them in bag with breadcrumbs. Shake to coat.
6. Pile pickles into air fryer basket and spray with oil.
7. Cook for 5 minutes. Shake basket and spray with oil.
8. Cook 5 more minutes. Shake and spray again. Separate any pickles that have stuck together and mist any spots you've missed.
9. Cook for 5 minutes longer or until dark golden brown and crispy.
10. **Variations & Ingredients Tips:**
11. Use panko breadcrumbs for a crunchier texture.
12. Add some garlic powder, onion powder or cayenne pepper to the breading.
13. Serve with ranch dressing, blue cheese dip or chipotle mayo for dipping.
14. **Per serving:** Calories: 265; Total Fat: 12g; Saturated Fat: 3g; Cholesterol: 93mg; Sodium: 1769mg; Total Carbs: 29g; Dietary Fiber: 2g; Total Sugars: 5g; Protein: 9g

Roasted Jalapeño Salsa Verde

Servings: 4
Prep Time: 10 Minutes | Cooking Time: 20 Minutes
Ingredients:
- 340 g fresh tomatillos, husked
- 1 jalapeño, stem removed
- 4 green onions, sliced
- 3 garlic cloves, peeled
- ½ tsp salt
- 1 tsp lime juice
- ¼ tsp apple cider vinegar
- ¼ cup cilantro leaves

Directions:
1. Preheat air fryer to 200°C/400°F. Add tomatillos and jalapeño to the frying basket and bake for 5 minutes. Put in green onions and garlic and bake for 5 more minutes. Transfer it into a food processor along with salt, lime juice, vinegar and cilantro and blend until the sauce is finely chopped. Pour it into a small sealable container and refrigerate it until ready to use up to five days.
2. **Variations & Ingredients Tips:**
3. Use serrano peppers or habaneros instead of jalapeños for a spicier salsa.
4. Add avocado for a creamier texture and flavor.
5. Grill the vegetables instead of air frying for a smokier taste.
6. **Per serving:** Calories: 41; Total Fat: 1g; Saturated Fat: 0g; Cholesterol: 0mg; Sodium: 296mg; Total Carbs: 8g; Dietary Fiber: 2g; Total Sugars: 4g; Protein: 1g

Corn Dog Muffins

Servings: 8
Prep Time: 15 Minutes | Cooking Time: 10 Minutes

Ingredients:
- 1¼ cups sliced kosher hotdogs (3 or 4, depending on size)
- ½ cup flour
- ½ cup yellow cornmeal
- 2 teaspoons baking powder
- ½ cup skim milk
- 1 egg
- 2 tablespoons canola oil
- 8 foil muffin cups, paper liners removed
- cooking spray
- mustard or your favorite dipping sauce

Directions:
1. Slice each hot dog in half lengthwise, then cut in 6 mm half-moon slices. Set aside.
2. Preheat air fryer to 200°C/390°F.
3. In a large bowl, stir together flour, cornmeal, and baking powder.
4. In a small bowl, beat together the milk, egg, and oil until just blended.
5. Pour egg mixture into dry **ingredient**s and stir with a spoon to mix well.
6. Stir in sliced hot dogs.
7. Spray the foil cups lightly with cooking spray.
8. Divide mixture evenly into muffin cups.
9. Place 4 muffin cups in the air fryer basket and cook for 5 minutes.
10. Reduce temperature to 180°C/360°F and cook 5 minutes or until toothpick inserted in center of muffin comes out clean.
11. Repeat steps 9 and 10 to bake remaining corn dog muffins.
12. Serve with mustard or other sauces for dipping.
13. **Variations & Ingredients Tips:**

14. Add some shredded cheddar cheese or diced jalapeños to the batter.
15. Use mini muffin cups for bite-sized corn dog poppers.
16. Brush the tops with melted butter and sprinkle with everything bagel seasoning before cooking.
17. **Per serving:** Calories: 177; Total Fat: 11g; Saturated Fat: 2g; Cholesterol: 41mg; Sodium: 398mg; Total Carbs: 13g; Dietary Fiber: 1g; Total Sugars: 1g; Protein: 6g

Beer Battered Onion Rings

Servings: 2
Prep Time: 20 Minutes | Cooking Time: 16 Minutes
Ingredients:
- 80 g flour
- ½ teaspoon baking soda
- 1 teaspoon paprika
- 1 teaspoon salt
- ½ teaspoon freshly ground black pepper
- 180 ml beer
- 1 egg, beaten
- 1½ cups fine breadcrumbs
- 1 large Vidalia onion, peeled and sliced into 13 mm rings
- vegetable oil

Directions:
1. Set up a dredging station. Mix the flour, baking soda, paprika, salt and pepper together in a bowl. Pour in the beer, add the egg and whisk until smooth. Place the breadcrumbs in a cake pan or shallow dish.
2. Separate the onion slices into individual rings. Dip each onion ring into the batter with a fork. Lift the onion ring out of the batter and let any excess batter drip off. Then place the onion ring in the breadcrumbs and shake the cake pan back

and forth to coat the battered onion ring. Pat the ring gently with your hands to make sure the breadcrumbs stick and that both sides of the ring are covered. Place the coated onion ring on a sheet pan and repeat with the rest of the onion rings.
3. Preheat the air fryer to 180°C/360°F.
4. Lightly spray the onion rings with oil, coating both sides. Layer the onion rings in the air fryer basket, stacking them on top of each other in a haphazard manner.
5. Air-fry for 10 minutes at 180°C/360°F. Flip the onion rings over and rotate the onion rings from the bottom of the basket to the top. Air-fry for an additional 6 minutes.
6. Serve immediately with your favorite dipping sauce.
7. **Variations & Ingredients Tips:**
8. Use sparkling water instead of beer for a non-alcoholic version.
9. Add some cayenne pepper or hot sauce to the batter for a spicy kick.
10. Serve with ranch dressing, chipotle mayo or marinara sauce for dipping.
11. **Per serving:** Calories: 456; Total Fat: 12g; Saturated Fat: 2g; Cholesterol: 93mg; Sodium: 1733mg; Total Carbs: 71g; Dietary Fiber: 5g; Total Sugars: 8g; Protein: 14g

Artichoke-spinach Dip

Servings: 4
Prep Time: 10 Minutes | Cooking Time: 25 Minutes
Ingredients:
- 113 g canned artichoke hearts, chopped
- ½ cup Greek yogurt
- ¼ cup cream cheese
- ½ cup spinach, chopped
- ½ red bell pepper, chopped
- 1 garlic clove, minced

- ½ tsp dried oregano
- 3 tsp grated Parmesan cheese

Directions:
1. Preheat air fryer to 170°C/340°F. Mix the yogurt and cream cheese. Add the artichoke, spinach, red bell pepper, garlic, and oregano, then put the mix in a pan and scatter Parmesan cheese on top. Put the pan in the frying basket and Bake for 9-14 minutes. The dip should be bubbly and brown. Serve hot.
2. **Variations & Ingredients Tips:**
3. Add some jalapeños or red pepper flakes for a spicy kick.
4. Top with shredded mozzarella before cooking for extra cheesiness.
5. Serve with sliced baguette, pita chips or fresh vegetables for dipping.
6. **Per serving:** Calories: 126; Total Fat: 9g; Saturated Fat: 5g; Cholesterol: 19mg; Sodium: 288mg; Total Carbs: 7g; Dietary Fiber: 2g; Total Sugars: 3g; Protein: 6g

Rumaki

Servings: 24
Prep Time: 20 Minutes | Cooking Time: 12 Minutes
Ingredients:
- 283 g raw chicken livers
- 1 can sliced water chestnuts, drained
- ¼ cup low-sodium teriyaki sauce
- 12 slices turkey bacon
- Toothpicks

Directions:

1. Cut livers into 3.8 cm pieces, trimming out tough veins as you slice. Place livers, water chestnuts, and teriyaki sauce in small container with lid. If needed, add another tablespoon of teriyaki sauce to make sure livers are covered. Refrigerate for 1 hour. When ready to cook, cut bacon slices in half crosswise. Wrap 1 piece of liver and 1 slice of water chestnut in each bacon strip. Secure with toothpick. When you have wrapped half of the livers, place them in the air fryer basket in a single layer. Cook at 200°C/390°F for 12 minutes, until liver is done and bacon is crispy. While first batch cooks, wrap the remaining livers. Repeat to cook your second batch.
2. **Variations** & **Tips**:
3. Use chicken gizzards instead of livers.
4. Marinate the livers overnight for more intense flavor.
5. Brush with additional teriyaki sauce after cooking.
6. **Per serving:** Calories: 69; Total Fat: 3g; Saturated Fat: 1g; Cholesterol: 150mg; Sodium: 206mg; Total Carbs: 2g; Dietary Fiber: 0g; Total Sugars: 1g; Protein: 8g

Spicy Pearl Onion Dip

Servings: 4
Prep Time: 15 Minutes | Cooking Time: 20 Minutes + Chilling Time
Ingredients:
- 2 cups peeled pearl onions
- 3 garlic cloves
- 3 tbsp olive oil
- Salt and pepper to taste
- 1 cup Greek yogurt
- ¼ tsp Worcestershire sauce
- 1 tbsp lemon juice
- ⅛ tsp red pepper flakes
- 1 tbsp chives, chopped

Directions:
1. Preheat air fryer to 180°C/360°F. Place the onions, garlic, and 2 tbsp of olive oil in a bowl and combine until the onions are well coated. Pour the mixture into the frying basket and roast for 11-13 minutes. Transfer the garlic and onions to your food processor. Pulse the vegetables several times until the onions are minced but still have some chunks. Combine the garlic and onions and the remaining olive oil, along with the salt, yogurt, Worcestershire sauce, lemon juice, black pepper, chives and red pepper flakes in a bowl. Cover and chill for at least 1 hour. Serve with toasted bread if desired.
2. **Variations & Ingredients Tips:**
3. Roast a few slices of bacon along with the onions and crumble them into the dip for a smoky flavor.
4. Add grated Parmesan cheese, sun-dried tomatoes, or pesto for an Italian twist.
5. Serve with crudités, pita chips, or crackers for dipping.
6. **Per Serving:** Calories: 178; Total Fat: 14g; Saturated Fat: 2g; Cholesterol: 3mg; Sodium: 68mg; Total Carbohydrates: 10g; Dietary Fiber: 1g; Total Sugars: 5g; Protein: 5g

Hot Cauliflower Bites

Servings: 4
Prep Time: 15 Minutes | Cooking Time: 35 Minutes
Ingredients:
- 1 head cauliflower, cut into florets
- 1 cup all-purpose flour
- 1 tsp garlic powder
- 1/3 cup cayenne sauce

Directions:
1. Preheat air fryer to 190°C/370°F. Mix the flour, 1 cup of water, and garlic powder in a large bowl until a batter forms.

Coat cauliflower in the batter, then transfer to a large bowl to drain excess. Place the cauliflower in the greased frying basket without stacking. Spray with cooking, then Bake for 6 minutes. Remove from the air fryer and transfer to a large bowl. Top with cayenne sauce. Return to the fryer and cook for 6 minutes or until crispy. Serve.
2. **Variations & Ingredients Tips:**
3. Use broccoli florets or zucchini chunks instead of cauliflower.
4. Toss the cooked bites with buffalo sauce, BBQ sauce or teriyaki glaze.
5. Serve with blue cheese dressing or ranch dip on the side.
6. **Per serving:** Calories: 154; Total Fat: 1g; Saturated Fat: 0g; Cholesterol: 0mg; Sodium: 613mg; Total Carbs: 33g; Dietary Fiber: 5g; Total Sugars: 3g; Protein: 6g

Poultry Recipes

Maple Bacon Wrapped Chicken Breasts

Servings: 2
Prep Time: 15 Minutes | Cooking Time: 18 Minutes
Ingredients:
- 2 (170g) boneless, skinless chicken breasts
- 2 tablespoons maple syrup, divided
- Freshly ground black pepper
- 6 slices thick-sliced bacon
- Fresh celery or parsley leaves
- Ranch Dressing:
- 1/4 cup mayonnaise
- 1/4 cup buttermilk
- 1/4 cup Greek yogurt
- 1 tablespoon chopped fresh chives
- 1 tablespoon chopped fresh parsley

- 1 tablespoon chopped fresh dill
- 1 tablespoon lemon juice
- Salt and freshly ground black pepper

Directions:
1. Brush the chicken breasts with half the maple syrup and season with freshly ground black pepper. Wrap three slices of bacon around each chicken breast, securing the ends with toothpicks.
2. Preheat the air fryer to 190°C/380°F.
3. Air-fry the chicken for 6 minutes. Then turn the chicken breasts over, pour more maple syrup on top and air-fry for another 6 minutes. Turn the chicken breasts one more time, brush the remaining maple syrup all over and continue to air-fry for a final 6 minutes.
4. While the chicken is cooking, prepare the dressing by combining all the dressing **ingredient**s together in a bowl.
5. When the chicken has finished cooking, remove the toothpicks and serve each breast with a little dressing drizzled over each one. Scatter lots of fresh celery or parsley leaves on top.
6. **Variations & Ingredients Tips:**
7. Use prosciutto or pancetta instead of bacon.
8. Stuff the chicken breasts with cheese or spinach before wrapping.
9. Serve with roasted sweet potatoes and green beans.
10. **Per serving:** Calories: 620; Total Fat: 41g; Saturated Fat: 12g; Cholesterol: 185mg; Sodium: 1200mg; Total Carbs: 14g; Dietary Fiber: 0g; Total Sugars: 11g; Protein: 51g

Fennel & Chicken Ratatouille

Servings: 4
Prep Time: 20 Minutes | Cooking Time: 30 Minutes
Ingredients:

- 450g boneless, skinless chicken thighs, cubed
- 2 tbsp grated Parmesan cheese
- 1 eggplant, cubed
- 1 zucchini, cubed
- 1 bell pepper, diced
- 1 fennel bulb, sliced
- 1 tsp salt
- 1 tsp Italian seasoning
- 2 tbsp olive oil
- 1 can (400g) diced tomatoes
- 1 tsp pasta sauce
- 2 tbsp basil leaves

Directions:
1. Preheat air fryer to 200°C/400°F.
2. Mix the chicken, eggplant, zucchini, bell pepper, fennel, salt, Italian seasoning, and oil in a bowl.
3. Place the chicken mixture in the frying basket and Air Fry for 7 minutes. Transfer it to a cake pan.
4. Mix in tomatoes along with juices and pasta sauce. Air Fry for 8 minutes.
5. Scatter with Parmesan and basil. Serve.
6. **Variations & Ingredients Tips:**
7. Use other vegetables like mushrooms, onions or summer squash.
8. Substitute fennel with celery for a milder flavor.
9. Serve over pasta, rice or with crusty bread.
10. **Per serving:** Calories: 320; Total Fat: 17g; Saturated Fat: 4g; Cholesterol: 105mg; Sodium: 820mg; Total Carbs: 16g; Dietary Fiber: 5g; Total Sugars: 8g; Protein: 27g

Sunday Chicken Skewers

Servings: 4
Prep Time: 15 Minutes | Cooking Time: 25 Minutes
Ingredients:
- 1 green bell pepper, cut into chunks
- 1 red bell pepper, cut into chunks
- 4 chicken breasts, cubed
- 1 tbsp chicken seasoning
- Salt and pepper to taste
- 16 cherry tomatoes
- 8 pearl onions, peeled

Directions:
1. Preheat air fryer to 180°C/360°F.
2. Season the chicken cubes with chicken seasoning, salt, and pepper.
3. Thread metal skewers with chicken, bell pepper chunks, cherry tomatoes, and pearl onions.
4. Put the kabobs in the greased frying basket.
5. Bake for 14-16 minutes, flipping once until cooked through.
6. Let cool slightly. Serve.
7. **Variations & Ingredients Tips:**
8. Use boneless, skinless chicken thighs for more flavor.
9. Marinate the chicken in Italian dressing before threading.
10. Add mushrooms, zucchini or pineapple chunks to the skewers.
11. Per Serving (2 skewers): Calories: 259; Total Fat: 4g; Saturated Fat: 1g; Cholesterol: 83mg; Sodium: 352mg; Total Carbs: 18g; Dietary Fiber: 3g; Total Sugars: 8g; Protein: 38g

Tandoori Chicken Legs

Servings: 2
Prep Time: 10 Minutes + Marinating | Cooking Time: 30 Minutes
Ingredients:
- 1 cup plain yogurt
- 2 cloves garlic, minced
- 1 tablespoon grated fresh ginger
- 2 teaspoons paprika
- 2 teaspoons ground coriander
- 1 teaspoon ground turmeric
- 1 teaspoon salt
- 1/4 teaspoon ground cayenne pepper
- Juice of 1 lime
- 2 bone-in, skin-on chicken legs
- Fresh cilantro leaves

Directions:
1. Make marinade by combining yogurt, garlic, ginger, spices and lime juice.
2. Slash chicken legs and pour marinade over them. Refrigerate for at least 1 hour.
3. Preheat air fryer to 195°C/380°F.
4. Transfer chicken from marinade to air fryer basket, reserving extra marinade.
5. Air fry for 15 mins. Flip chicken and pour over remaining marinade.
6. Air fry 15 more mins, tenting with foil if browning too much.
7. Serve over rice with fresh cilantro.
8. **Variations & Ingredients Tips:**
9. Use chicken thighs or breasts instead of legs.
10. Add a dollop of yogurt or cream to finished dish for richness.
11. Adjust cayenne amount to preference for heat level.
12. Per Serving (1 leg): Calories: 307; Total Fat: 13g; Saturated Fat: 4g; Cholesterol: 122mg; Sodium: 791mg; Total Carbs: 12g; Dietary Fiber: 1g; Total Sugars: 3g; Protein: 34g

Smoky Chicken Fajita Bowl

Servings: 4
Prep Time: 10 Minutes (plus 30 Minutes Chilling Time) | Cooking Time: 35 Minutes + Chilling Time

Ingredients:
- 1 jalapeño, sliced and seeded
- ½ cup queso fresco crumbles
- 1 tbsp olive oil
- 2 tsp flour
- ¼ tsp chili powder
- ¼ tsp fajita seasoning
- ¼ tsp smoked paprika
- ¼ tsp ground cumin
- ½ tsp granular honey
- ⅛ tsp onion powder
- ⅛ tsp garlic powder
- 454 grams chicken breast strips
- 4 tomatoes, diced
- ½ diced red onion
- 4 tbsp sour cream
- 1 avocado, diced

Directions:
1. Combine the olive oil, flour, all the spices, and chicken strips in a bowl. Let chill in the fridge for 30 minutes.
2. Preheat air fryer to 200°C/400°F.
3. Place the chicken strips in the air fryer basket and Air Fry for 8 minutes, shaking once.
4. Divide between 4 medium bowls. Add tomatoes, jalapeño, onion, queso fresco, sour cream, and avocado to the bowls.
5. Serve right away.
6. **Variations & Ingredients Tips:**

7. Use boneless, skinless chicken thighs instead of breasts for juicier meat.
8. Add sliced bell peppers, corn, or black beans to the bowls for extra veggies and fiber.
9. Serve with a side of salsa, guacamole, or tortilla chips for dipping.
10. **Per Serving:** Calories: 400; Total Fat: 23g; Saturated Fat: 7g; Sodium: 390mg; Total Carbohydrates: 15g; Dietary Fiber: 5g; Total Sugars: 6g; Protein: 37g

Satay Chicken Skewers

Servings: 4
Prep Time: 20 Minutes (plus 15 Minutes Marinating Time) | Cooking Time: 35 Minutes

Ingredients:
- 2 chicken breasts, cut into strips
- 1 ½ tbsp Thai red curry paste
- ¼ cup peanut butter
- 1 tbsp maple syrup
- 1 tbsp tamari
- 1 tbsp lime juice
- 2 tsp chopped onions
- ¼ tsp minced ginger
- 1 clove garlic, minced
- 1 cup coconut milk
- 1 tsp fish sauce
- 1 tbsp chopped cilantro

Directions:
1. Mix the peanut butter, maple syrup, tamari, lime juice, ¼ tsp of sriracha, onions, ginger, garlic, and 2 tbsp of water in a bowl. Reserve 1 tbsp of the sauce. Set aside.

2. Combine the reserved peanut sauce, fish sauce, coconut milk, Thai red curry paste, cilantro and chicken strips in a bowl and let marinate in the fridge for 15 minutes.
3. Preheat air fryer at 180°C/350°F.
4. Thread chicken strips onto skewers and place them on a kebab rack. Place rack in the air fryer basket and Air Fry for 12 minutes.
5. Serve with previously prepared peanut sauce on the side.
6. **Variations & Ingredients Tips:**
7. Use beef, pork, or shrimp instead of chicken for different protein options.
8. Add sliced bell peppers, onions, or mushrooms to the skewers for extra veggies.
9. Serve with steamed rice, cucumber salad, and lime wedges on the side.
10. **Per Serving:** Calories: 370; Total Fat: 24g; Saturated Fat: 13g; Sodium: 790mg; Total Carbohydrates: 13g; Dietary Fiber: 2g; Total Sugars: 7g; Protein: 30g

Chicken Burgers With Blue Cheese Sauce

Servings: 4
Prep Time: 15 Minutes | Cooking Time: 40 Minutes
Ingredients:
- ¼ cup crumbled blue cheese
- ¼ cup sour cream
- 2 tbsp mayonnaise
- 1 tbsp red hot sauce
- Salt to taste
- 3 tbsp buffalo wing sauce
- 454 grams ground chicken
- 2 tbsp grated carrot
- 2 tbsp diced celery
- 1 egg white

Directions:
1. Whisk the blue cheese, sour cream, mayonnaise, red hot sauce, salt, and 1 tbsp of buffalo sauce in a bowl. Let sit covered in the fridge until ready to use.
2. Preheat air fryer at 180°C/350°F.
3. In another bowl, combine the remaining **ingredient**s. Form mixture into 4 patties, making a slight indentation in the middle of each.
4. Place patties in the greased air fryer basket and Air Fry for 13 minutes until you reach your desired doneness, flipping once.
5. Serve with the blue cheese sauce.
6. **Variations & Ingredients Tips:**
7. Use ground turkey or beef instead of chicken for different flavors.
8. Add diced jalapeños or hot sauce to the patty mixture for extra heat.
9. Serve on a bun with lettuce, tomato, and pickles for a complete burger.
10. **Per Serving:** Calories: 340; Total Fat: 24g; Saturated Fat: 8g; Sodium: 1080mg; Total Carbohydrates: 4g; Dietary Fiber: 0g; Total Sugars: 2g; Protein: 27g

Cheesy Chicken-avocado Paninis

Servings: 2
Prep Time: 15 Minutes | Cooking Time: 25 Minutes
Ingredients:
- 2 tbsp mayonnaise
- 4 tsp yellow mustard
- 4 sandwich bread slices
- 113 grams sliced deli chicken ham
- 57 grams sliced provolone cheese
- 57 grams sliced mozzarella

- 1 avocado, sliced
- 1 tomato, sliced
- Salt and pepper to taste
- 1 tsp sesame seeds
- 2 tbsp butter, melted

Directions:
1. Preheat air fryer at 180°C/350°F.
2. Rub mayonnaise and mustard on the inside of each bread slice.
3. Top 2 bread slices with chicken ham, provolone and mozzarella cheese, avocado, sesame seeds, and tomato slices. Season with salt and pepper. Then, close sandwiches with the remaining bread slices.
4. Brush the top and bottom of each sandwich lightly with melted butter.
5. Place sandwiches in the air fryer basket and Bake for 6 minutes, flipping once.
6. Serve.
7. **Variations & Ingredients Tips:**
8. Substitute chicken ham with sliced turkey, roast beef, or bacon.
9. Use pesto, hummus, or guacamole instead of mayonnaise and mustard.
10. Add sliced onions, bell peppers, or pickles for extra crunch and flavor.
11. **Per Serving:** Calories: 680; Total Fat: 49g; Saturated Fat: 20g; Sodium: 1460mg; Total Carbohydrates: 32g; Dietary Fiber: 6g; Total Sugars: 6g; Protein: 32g

Chicken Parmigiana

Servings: 2
Prep Time: 10 Minutes | Cooking Time: 35 Minutes

Ingredients:
- 2 chicken breasts
- 1 cup breadcrumbs
- 2 eggs, beaten
- Salt and pepper to taste
- 1 tbsp dried basil
- 1 cup passata
- 2 provolone cheese slices
- 1 tbsp Parmesan cheese

Directions:
1. Preheat air fryer to 175°C/350°F.
2. Mix breadcrumbs, basil, salt and pepper in a bowl.
3. Coat chicken in breadcrumb mixture, then egg, then breadcrumbs again.
4. Arrange coated chicken in greased air fryer basket.
5. Air fry for 20 mins, flipping halfway through.
6. Pour half the passata into a baking pan. Place cooked chicken over it.
7. Top with remaining passata, provolone and parmesan.
8. Bake for 5 more mins until cheese is melted.
9. Serve hot.
10. **Variations & Ingredients Tips:**
11. Use marinara sauce instead of passata.
12. Add garlic powder or Italian herbs to the breadcrumb mixture.
13. Serve over pasta or with roasted vegetables.
14. **Per Serving:** Calories: 574; Total Fat: 18g; Saturated Fat: 8g; Cholesterol: 256mg; Sodium: 947mg; Total Carbs: 51g; Dietary Fiber: 3g; Total Sugars: 6g; Protein: 51g

Thai Chicken Drumsticks

Servings: 4

Prep Time: 10 Minutes + Marinating | Cooking Time: 20 Minutes
Ingredients:
- 2 tablespoons soy sauce
- 1/4 cup rice wine vinegar
- 2 tablespoons chili garlic sauce
- 2 tablespoons sesame oil
- 1 teaspoon minced fresh ginger
- 2 teaspoons sugar
- 1/2 teaspoon ground coriander
- Juice of 1 lime
- 8 chicken drumsticks (about 1.1kg)
- 1/4 cup chopped peanuts
- Chopped fresh cilantro
- Lime wedges

Directions:
1. Combine soy sauce, vinegar, chili sauce, oil, ginger, sugar, coriander and lime juice. Add drumsticks and marinate 30 mins.
2. Preheat air fryer to 190°C/370°F.
3. Place chicken in basket, spooning over half the marinade and reserving half.
4. Air fry 10 mins, turn and pour over remaining marinade. Cook 10 more mins.
5. Transfer chicken to plate and simmer marinade in a pan for 2 mins until thickened.
6. Serve chicken with thickened sauce, chopped peanuts, cilantro and lime wedges.
7. **Variations & Ingredients Tips:**
8. Use chicken thighs instead of drumsticks.
9. Add fish sauce or curry paste to the marinade.
10. Serve over rice noodles or with a fresh salad.
11. Per Serving (2 drumsticks): Calories: 440; Total Fat: 27g; Saturated Fat: 6g; Cholesterol: 165mg; Sodium: 846mg; Total Carbs: 11g; Dietary Fiber: 1g; Total Sugars: 6g; Protein: 38g

Beef, Pork & Lamb Recipes

Blossom Bbq Pork Chops

Servings: 2
Prep Time: 10 Minutes | Cooking Time: 20 Minutes
Ingredients:
- 2 tbsp cherry preserves
- 1 tbsp honey
- 1 tbsp Dijon mustard
- 2 tsp light brown sugar
- 1 tsp Worcestershire sauce
- 1 tbsp lime juice
- 1 tbsp olive oil
- 2 cloves garlic, minced
- 1 tbsp chopped parsley
- 2 pork chops

Directions:
1. Mix all **ingredient**s except pork chops in a bowl. Add pork chops and marinate covered in the fridge for 30 minutes.
2. Preheat air fryer to 177°C/350°F.
3. Place pork chops in the greased basket and air fry for 12 minutes at 177°C/350°F, turning once.
4. Let rest for 5 minutes before serving.
5. **Variations & Ingredients Tips:**
6. Use bone-in or boneless pork chops
7. Substitute orange juice for the lime juice
8. Add 1 tsp smoked paprika or chipotle powder for a smoky flavor
9. **Per Serving:** Calories: 310; Total Fat: 12g; Saturated Fat: 3g; Cholesterol: 85mg; Sodium: 470mg; Total Carbs: 20g; Fiber: 1g; Sugars: 14g; Protein: 28g

Leftover Roast Beef Risotto

Servings: 4
Prep Time: 10 Minutes | Cooking Time: 30 Minutes
Ingredients:
- ½ chopped red bell pepper
- ½ chopped cooked roast beef
- 3 tablespoons grated Parmesan
- 2 teaspoons butter, melted
- 1 shallot, finely chopped
- 3 garlic cloves, minced
- ¾ cup short-grain rice
- 1¼ cups beef broth

Directions:
1. Preheat air fryer to 200°C/390°F. Add the melted butter, shallot, garlic, and red bell pepper to a baking pan and stir to combine. Air Fry for 2 minutes, or until the vegetables are crisp-tender.
2. Remove from the air fryer and stir in the rice, broth, and roast beef.
3. Put the cooking pan back into the fryer and Bake for 18-22 minutes, stirring once during cooking until the rice is al dente and the beef is cooked through.
4. Sprinkle with Parmesan and serve.
5. **Variations & Ingredients Tips:**
6. Use different types of cheese, such as Gruyère or Asiago, for a variety of flavors.
7. Add some sliced mushrooms or peas to the risotto for extra vegetables.
8. Serve the risotto with a side of roasted asparagus or a green salad for a complete meal.

9. **Per Serving:** Calories: 280; Total Fat: 10g; Saturated Fat: 5g; Cholesterol: 45mg; Sodium: 530mg; Total Carbs: 29g; Fiber: 1g; Sugars: 2g; Protein: 17g

Rib Eye Cheesesteaks With Fried Onions

Servings: 2
Prep Time: 15 Minutes | Cooking Time: 20 Minutes
Ingredients:
- 1 (340 g) rib eye steak
- 2 tablespoons Worcestershire sauce
- salt and freshly ground black pepper
- ½ onion, sliced
- 2 tablespoons butter, melted
- 113 g sliced Cheddar or provolone cheese
- 2 long hoagie rolls, lightly toasted

Directions:
1. Place the steak in the freezer for 30 minutes to make it easier to slice. When it is well-chilled, thinly slice the steak against the grain and transfer it to a bowl. Pour the Worcestershire sauce over the steak and season it with salt and pepper. Allow the meat to come to room temperature.
2. Preheat the air fryer to 200°C/400°F.
3. Toss the sliced onion with the butter and transfer it to the air fryer basket. Air-fry at 200°C/400°F for 12 minutes, shaking the basket a few times during the cooking process. Place the steak on top of the onions and air-fry for another 6 minutes, stirring the meat and onions together halfway through the cooking time.
4. When the air fryer has finished cooking, divide the steak and onions in half in the air fryer basket, pushing each half to one side of the air fryer basket. Place the cheese on top of

each half, push the drawer back into the turned off air fryer and let it sit for 2 minutes, until the cheese has melted.
5. Transfer each half of the cheesesteak mixture into a toasted roll with the cheese side up and dig in!
6. **Variations & Ingredients Tips:**
7. Add some sautéed mushrooms or bell peppers to the sandwiches
8. Use Swiss cheese or spicy pepper Jack for different flavors
9. Spread some garlic aioli or hot sauce on the rolls before filling
10. **Per Serving:** Calories: 835; Total Fat: 56g; Saturated Fat: 29g; Cholesterol: 175mg; Sodium: 970mg; Total Carbs: 34g; Dietary Fiber: 2g; Total Sugars: 5g; Protein: 52g

Steak Fajitas

Servings: 4
Prep Time: 15 Minutes | Cooking Time: 20 Minutes
Ingredients:
- 454 g beef flank steak, cut into strips
- 1 red bell pepper, cut into strips
- 1 green bell pepper, cut into strips
- 118 g sweet corn
- 1 shallot, cut into strips
- 2 tablespoons fajita seasoning
- Salt and pepper to taste
- 2 tablespoons olive oil
- 8 flour tortillas

Directions:
1. Preheat air fryer to 190°C/380°F. Combine beef, bell peppers, corn, shallot, fajita seasoning, salt, pepper, and olive oil in a large bowl until well mixed.

2. Pour the beef and vegetable mixture into the air fryer. Air Fry for 9-11 minutes, shaking the basket once halfway through. Spoon a portion of the beef and vegetables in each of the tortillas and top with favorite toppings. Serve.
3. **Variations & Ingredients Tips:**
4. Use chicken breast or shrimp instead of steak for a change
5. Add some sliced jalapeños or hot sauce for spicy kick
6. Serve with guacamole, sour cream, salsa and lime wedges
7. **Per Serving:** Calories: 514; Total Fat: 22g; Saturated Fat: 6g; Cholesterol: 68mg; Sodium: 1007mg; Total Carbs: 49g; Dietary Fiber: 4g; Total Sugars: 4g; Protein: 32g

Venison Backstrap

Servings: 4
Prep Time: 15 Minutes | Cooking Time: 10 Minutes
Ingredients:
- 2 eggs
- 1/4 cup milk
- 1 cup whole wheat flour
- 1/2 teaspoon salt
- 1/4 teaspoon pepper
- 454g venison backstrap, sliced
- Salt and pepper
- Oil for misting or cooking spray

Directions:
1. Beat together eggs and milk in a shallow dish.
2. In another shallow dish, combine the flour, salt, and pepper. Stir to mix well.
3. Sprinkle venison steaks with additional salt and pepper to taste. Dip in flour, egg wash, then in flour again, pressing in coating.
4. Spray steaks with oil or cooking spray on both sides.

5. Cooking in 2 batches, place steaks in the air fryer basket in a single layer. Cook at 360°F/182°C for 8 minutes. Spray with oil, turn over, and spray other side. Cook for 2 minutes longer, until coating is crispy brown and meat is done to your liking.
6. Repeat to cook remaining venison.
7. **Variations & Ingredients Tips:**
8. Use breadcrumbs or crushed pork rinds instead of flour for keto/low-carb
9. Add cajun or blackening seasoning to the flour coating for a kick
10. Serve with mushroom or pepper gravy on the side
11. **Per Serving:** Calories: 295; Total Fat: 9g; Saturated Fat: 3g; Cholesterol: 160mg; Sodium: 390mg; Total Carbs: 18g; Dietary Fiber: 2g; Total Sugars: 1g; Protein: 34g

Carne Asada

Servings: 3
Prep Time: 20 Minutes | Cooking Time: 12 Minutes
Ingredients:
- 1/4 cup Orange juice
- 3 tablespoons Regular or low-sodium soy sauce or gluten-free tamari sauce
- 1 1/2 tablespoons Lemon juice
- 1 1/2 tablespoons Lime juice
- 1 1/2 teaspoons Minced garlic
- 3/4 teaspoon Ground cumin
- 3/4 teaspoon Dried oregano
- Up to 3/4 teaspoon Red pepper flakes
- 340g Beef skirt steak

Directions:

1. Mix the orange juice, soy or tamari sauce, lemon juice, lime juice, garlic, cumin, oregano, and red pepper flakes in a large bowl. Add the steak and turn several time to coat. Cover and refrigerate for at least 2 hours or up to 6 hours, turning the meat in the marinade twice or more.
2. Preheat the air fryer to 205°C/400°F.
3. Meanwhile, remove the steak from the marinade, discard any remaining marinade, and cut the steak into pieces that will fit in the basket in one layer. Leave these out at room temperature as the machine heats.
4. When the machine is at temperature, set the steak pieces in the basket, overlapping them as necessary without letting any climb up the side of the basket. Air-fry for 12 minutes, turning and rearranging the pieces once so that any covered bits are exposed, until browned and sizzling.
5. Use kitchen tongs to transfer the pieces of skirt steak to a cutting board. Cool for 5 minutes, then carve against the grain into 1.3-cm-thick strips.
6. **Variations & Ingredients Tips:**
7. Use orange juice or pineapple juice instead of lemon/lime for a different flavor
8. Add honey or brown sugar to the marinade for a sweet/spicy glaze
9. Toss in sliced onions and bell peppers to the air fryer for fajita-style steak
10. **Per serving:** Calories: 280; Total Fat: 14g; Saturated Fat: 5g; Cholesterol: 90mg; Sodium: 670mg; Total Carbohydrates: 7g; Dietary Fiber: 0g; Total Sugars: 5g; Protein: 31g

Beef & Spinach Sautée

Servings: 4
Prep Time: 10 Minutes | Cooking Time: 30 Minutes
Ingredients:
- 2 tomatoes, chopped

- 2 tbsp crumbled goat cheese
- 225 g ground beef
- 1 shallot, chopped
- 2 garlic cloves, minced
- 2 cups baby spinach
- 2 tbsp lemon juice
- 80 ml beef broth

Directions:
1. Preheat air fryer to 190°C/370°F. Crumble the beef in a baking pan and place it in the air fryer. Air fry for 3-7 minutes, stirring once. Drain the meat and make sure it's browned. Toss in the tomatoes, shallot, and garlic and air fry for an additional 4-8 minutes until soft. Toss in the spinach, lemon juice, and beef broth and cook for 2-4 minutes until the spinach wilts. Top with goat cheese and serve.
2. **Variations & Ingredients Tips:**
3. Use ground turkey, chicken, or pork instead of beef for a leaner option.
4. Add sliced mushrooms, bell peppers, or zucchini for extra veggies.
5. Serve over rice, quinoa, or pasta for a heartier meal.
6. **Per Serving:** Calories: 215; Total Fat: 13g; Saturated Fat: 6g; Cholesterol: 56mg; Sodium: 253mg; Total Carbohydrates: 6g; Dietary Fiber: 2g; Total Sugars: 3g; Protein: 17g

Smokehouse-style Beef Ribs

Servings: 3
Prep Time: 5 Minutes | Cooking Time: 25 Minutes
Ingredients:
- 1 g Mild smoked paprika
- 1 g Garlic powder
- 1 g Onion powder

- 1 g Table salt
- 1 g Ground black pepper
- 3 283 g to 340 g beef back ribs (not beef short ribs)

Directions:
1. Preheat the air fryer to 175°C/350°F.
2. Mix the smoked paprika, garlic powder, onion powder, salt, and pepper in a small bowl until uniform. Massage and pat this mixture onto the ribs.
3. When the machine is at temperature, set the ribs in the basket in one layer, turning them on their sides if necessary, sort of like they're spooning but with at least 6 mm air space between them. Air-fry for 25 minutes, turning once, until deep brown and sizzling.
4. Use kitchen tongs to transfer the ribs to a wire rack. Cool for 5 minutes before serving.
5. **Variations & Ingredients Tips:**
6. Brush the ribs with your favorite BBQ sauce in the last 5 minutes of cooking
7. Sprinkle with chopped parsley or green onions before serving
8. Serve with coleslaw, potato salad and cornbread for a BBQ feast
9. **Per Serving:** Calories: 456; Total Fat: 35g; Saturated Fat: 14g; Cholesterol: 113mg; Sodium: 378mg; Total Carbs: 1g; Dietary Fiber: 0g; Total Sugars: 0g; Protein: 32g

Classic Salisbury Steak Burgers

Servings: 4
Prep Time: 15 Minutes | Cooking Time: 35 Minutes
Ingredients:
- ¼ cup bread crumbs
- 2 tablespoons beef broth
- 1 tablespoon cooking sherry

- 1 tablespoon ketchup
- 1 tablespoon Dijon mustard
- 2 teaspoons Worcestershire sauce
- ½ teaspoon onion powder
- ½ teaspoon garlic powder
- 450 g ground beef
- 1 cup sliced mushrooms
- 1 tablespoon butter
- 4 buns, split and toasted

Directions:
1. Preheat the air fryer to 190°C/375°F.
2. Combine the bread crumbs, broth, cooking sherry, ketchup, mustard, Worcestershire sauce, garlic and onion powder and mix well. Add the beef and mix with hands, then form into 4 patties and refrigerate while preparing the mushrooms.
3. Mix the mushrooms and butter in a 15 cm pan. Place the pan in the air fryer and Bake for 8-10 minutes, stirring once until the mushrooms are brown and tender. Remove and set aside.
4. Line the frying basket with round parchment paper and punch holes in it. Lay the burgers in a single layer and cook for 11-14 minutes or until cooked through.
5. Put the burgers on the bun bottoms, top with the mushrooms, then the bun tops.
6. **Variations & Ingredients Tips:**
7. Use different types of mushrooms, such as shiitake or cremini, for a variety of flavors and textures.
8. Add some sliced onions or bell peppers to the mushroom mixture for extra vegetables.
9. Serve the Salisbury steak burgers with a side of mashed potatoes or green beans for a classic comfort food meal.
10. **Per Serving:** Calories: 430; Total Fat: 23g; Saturated Fat: 9g; Cholesterol: 105mg; Sodium: 670mg; Total Carbs: 26g; Fiber: 2g; Sugars: 5g; Protein: 31g

Sirloin Steak Bites With Gravy

Servings: 4
Prep Time: 10 Minutes | Cooking Time: 20 Minutes
Ingredients:
- 680 g sirloin steak, cubed
- 1 tablespoon olive oil
- 2 tablespoons cornstarch, divided
- 2 tablespoons soy sauce
- 2 tablespoons Worcestershire sauce
- 2 garlic cloves, minced
- Salt and pepper to taste
- ½ teaspoon smoked paprika
- ½ cup sliced red onion
- 2 fresh thyme sprigs
- ½ cup sliced mushrooms
- 1 cup beef broth
- 1 tablespoon butter

Directions:
1. Preheat air fryer to 200°C/400°F. Combine beef, olive oil, 1 tablespoon of cornstarch, garlic, pepper, Worcestershire sauce, soy sauce, thyme, salt, and paprika. Arrange the beef on the greased baking dish, then top with onions and mushrooms. Place the dish in the frying basket and bake for 4 minutes. While the beef is baking, whisk beef broth and the rest of the cornstarch in a small bowl. When the beef is ready, add butter and beef broth to the baking dish. Bake for another 5 minutes. Allow resting for 5 minutes. Serve and enjoy.
2. **Variations & Ingredients Tips:**
3. Use chuck roast or stew meat instead of sirloin
4. Add some baby potatoes or carrots to the dish
5. Serve over mashed potatoes, egg noodles or rice
6. **Per Serving:** Calories: 382; Total Fat: 20g; Saturated Fat: 7g; Cholesterol: 122mg; Sodium: 809mg; Total Carbs: 8g; Dietary Fiber: 1g; Total Sugars: 2g; Protein: 41g

Fish And Seafood Recipes

Classic Crab Cakes

Servings: 4
Prep Time: 15 Minutes | Cooking Time: 10 Minutes
Ingredients:
- 280g lump crabmeat, picked over for shell and cartilage
- 6 tablespoons plain panko bread crumbs (gluten-free, if a concern)
- 6 tablespoons chopped drained jarred roasted red peppers
- 4 medium scallions, trimmed and thinly sliced
- 1/4 cup regular or low-fat mayonnaise (not fat-free; gluten-free, if a concern)
- 1/4 teaspoon dried dill
- 1/4 teaspoon dried thyme
- 1/4 teaspoon onion powder
- 1/4 teaspoon table salt
- 1/8 teaspoon celery seeds
- Up to 1/8 teaspoon cayenne
- Vegetable oil spray

Directions:
1. Preheat the air fryer to 200°C/400°F.
2. Gently mix the crabmeat, bread crumbs, red pepper, scallion, mayonnaise, dill, thyme, onion powder, salt, celery seeds, and cayenne in a bowl until well combined.
3. Use clean and dry hands to form 1/2 cup of this mixture into a tightly packed 2.5-cm-thick, 7.5- to 10-cm-wide patty. Coat the top and bottom of the patty with vegetable oil spray and

set it aside. Continue making 1 more patty for a small batch, 3 more for a medium batch, or 5 more for a larger one, coating them with vegetable oil spray on both sides.
4. Set the patties in one layer in the basket and air-fry undisturbed for 10 minutes, or until lightly browned and cooked through.
5. Use a nonstick-safe spatula to transfer the crab cakes to a serving platter or plates. Wait a couple of minutes before serving.
6. **Variations & Ingredients Tips:**
7. Add some Old Bay seasoning or Cajun spice to the mix.
8. Form into mini crab cakes and serve as an appetizer.
9. Serve with a lemon-caper aioli or spicy remoulade sauce.
10. **Per serving:** Calories: 200; Total Fat: 12g; Saturated Fat: 2.5g; Cholesterol: 85mg; Sodium: 720mg; Total Carbs: 10g; Dietary Fiber: 1g; Total Sugars: 2g; Protein: 15g

Spiced Shrimp Empanadas

Servings: 5
Prep Time: 15 Minutes | Cooking Time: 30 Minutes
Ingredients:
- 225g peeled and deveined shrimp, chopped
- 2 tbsp diced red bell peppers
- 1 shallot, minced
- 1 scallion, chopped
- 2 garlic cloves, minced
- 2 tbsp chopped cilantro
- 1/2 tbsp lemon juice
- 1/4 tsp sweet paprika
- 1/8 tsp salt
- 1/8 tsp red pepper flakes
- 1/4 tsp ground nutmeg
- 1 large egg, beaten
- 10 empanada discs

Directions:
1. Combine all **ingredient**s except egg and discs in a bowl.
2. Beat egg with 1 tsp water in a small bowl.
3. Place 2 tbsp shrimp filling in center of each disc.
4. Brush edges with egg wash and fold in half to seal. Crimp with a fork.
5. Brush tops with egg wash.
6. Preheat air fryer to 190°C/380°F.
7. Place empanadas in greased basket. Air Fry 9 mins, flipping once, until golden.
8. Serve hot.
9. **Variations & Ingredients Tips:**
10. Use pie crust dough instead of empanada discs.
11. Add shredded cheese to the filling.
12. Serve with guacamole or sour cream for dipping.
13. **Per serving:** Calories: 180; Total Fat: 6g; Saturated Fat: 1g; Cholesterol: 95mg; Sodium: 280mg; Total Carbs: 22g; Dietary Fiber: 1g; Sugars: 1g; Protein: 10g

Crabmeat-stuffed Flounder

Servings: 3
Prep Time: 20 Minutes | Cooking Time: 12 Minutes
Ingredients:
- 130g purchased backfin or claw crabmeat, picked over for bits of shell and cartilage
- 6 saltine crackers, crushed into fine crumbs
- 2 tablespoons plus 1 teaspoon regular or low-fat mayonnaise (not fat-free)
- 3/4 teaspoon yellow prepared mustard
- 1 1/2 teaspoons Worcestershire sauce
- 1/8 teaspoon celery salt
- 3 (140-170g) skinless flounder fillets

- Vegetable oil spray
- Mild paprika

Directions:
1. Preheat the air fryer to 200°C/400°F.
2. Gently mix the crabmeat, crushed saltines, mayonnaise, mustard, Worcestershire sauce, and celery salt in a bowl until well combined.
3. Generously coat the flat side of a fillet with vegetable oil spray. Set the fillet sprayed side down on your work surface. Cut the fillet in half widthwise, then cut one of the halves in half lengthwise. Set a scant 1/3 cup of the crabmeat mixture on top of the undivided half of the fish fillet, mounding the mixture to make an oval that somewhat fits the shape of the fillet with at least a 6-mm border of fillet beyond the filling all around.
4. Take the two thin divided quarters (that is, the halves of the half) and lay them lengthwise over the filling, overlapping at each end and leaving a little space in the middle where the filling peeks through. Coat the top of the stuffed flounder piece with vegetable oil spray, then sprinkle paprika over the stuffed flounder fillet. Set aside and use the remaining fillet(s) to make more stuffed flounder "packets," repeating steps 3 and
5. Use a nonstick-safe spatula to transfer the stuffed flounder fillets to the basket. Leave as much space between them as possible. Air-fry undisturbed for 12 minutes, or until lightly brown and firm (but not hard).
6. Use that same spatula, plus perhaps another one, to transfer the fillets to a serving platter or plates. Cool for a minute or two, then serve hot.
7. **Variations & Ingredients Tips:**
8. Stuff with shrimp or lobster meat instead of crab.
9. Sprinkle with Old Bay seasoning in addition to the paprika.
10. Serve with a lemon beurre blanc or hollandaise sauce.
11. **Per serving:** Calories: 250; Total Fat: 10g; Saturated Fat: 1.5g; Cholesterol: 140mg; Sodium: 660mg; Total Carbs: 9g; Dietary Fiber: 0g; Total Sugars: 1g; Protein: 31g

Corn & Shrimp Boil

Servings: 4
Prep Time: 15 Minutes | Cooking Time: 40 Minutes
Ingredients:
- 8 frozen "mini" corn on the cob
- 1 tbsp smoked paprika
- 2 tsp dried thyme
- 1 tsp dried marjoram
- 1 tsp sea salt
- 1 tsp garlic powder
- 1 tsp onion powder
- 1 tsp cayenne pepper
- 450g baby potatoes, halved
- 1 tbsp olive oil
- 450g peeled shrimp, deveined
- 1 avocado, sliced

Directions:
1. Preheat the air fryer to 190°C/370°F.
2. Combine the paprika, thyme, marjoram, salt, garlic, onion, and cayenne and mix well. Pour into a small glass jar.
3. Add the potatoes, corn, and olive oil to the frying basket and sprinkle with 2 tsp of the spice mix and toss. Air Fry for 15 minutes, shaking the basket once until tender. Remove and set aside.
4. Put the shrimp in the frying basket and sprinkle with 2 tsp of the spice mix. Air Fry for 5-8 minutes, shaking once until shrimp are tender and pink.
5. Combine all the **ingredient**s in the frying basket and sprinkle with 2 tsp of the spice mix. Toss to coat and cook for 1-2 more minutes or until hot.
6. Serve topped with avocado.
7. **Variations & Ingredients Tips:**

8. Add some sliced andouille sausage or bacon to the mix.
9. Squeeze some lemon juice over the top before serving.
10. Sprinkle with chopped fresh parsley or dill.
11. **Per serving:** Calories: 380; Total Fat: 16g; Saturated Fat: 2.5g; Cholesterol: 180mg; Sodium: 1220mg; Total Carbs: 40g; Dietary Fiber: 8g; Total Sugars: 5g; Protein: 27g

Mediterranean Salmon Cakes

Servings: 4
Prep Time: 15 Minutes | Cooking Time: 30 Minutes
Ingredients:
- 1/4 cup heavy cream
- 5 tbsp mayonnaise
- 2 cloves garlic, minced
- 1/4 tsp caper juice
- 2 tsp lemon juice
- 1 tbsp capers
- 1 can salmon
- 2 tsp lemon zest
- 1 egg
- 1/4 minced red bell peppers
- 1/2 cup flour
- 1/8 tsp salt
- 2 tbsp sliced green olives

Directions:
1. Combine heavy cream, 2 tbsp mayonnaise, garlic, caper juices, capers, and lemon juice in a bowl. Place the resulting caper sauce in the fridge until ready to use.
2. Preheat air fryer to 200°C/400°F.

3. Combine canned salmon, lemon zest, egg, remaining mayonnaise, bell peppers, flour, and salt in a bowl. Form into 8 patties.
4. Place the patties in the greased frying basket and Air Fry for 10 minutes, turning once.
5. Let rest for 5 minutes before drizzling with lemon sauce. Garnish with green olives to serve.
6. **Variations & Ingredients Tips:**
7. Use fresh salmon instead of canned.
8. Add breadcrumbs or panko to the patty mixture to bind.
9. Serve on a bed of greens or with roasted veggies.
10. **Per serving:** Calories: 375, Total Fat: 27g, Saturated Fat: 6g, Cholesterol: 135mg, Sodium: 530mg, Total Carbs: 16g, Fiber: 1g, Sugars: 2g, Protein: 18g

Feta & Shrimp Pita

Servings: 4
Prep Time: 10 Minutes | Cooking Time: 15 Minutes
Ingredients:
- 450g peeled shrimp, deveined
- 2 tbsp olive oil
- 1 tsp dried oregano
- 1/2 tsp dried thyme
- 1/2 tsp garlic powder
- 1/4 tsp shallot powder
- 1/4 tsp tarragon powder
- Salt and pepper to taste
- 4 whole-wheat pitas
- 115g feta cheese, crumbled
- 1 cup grated lettuce
- 1 tomato, diced
- 1/4 cup black olives, sliced
- 1 lemon

Directions:
1. Preheat oven to 195°C/380°F.
2. Mix shrimp with oil, oregano, thyme, garlic, shallot, tarragon powders, salt and pepper.
3. Pour shrimp in air fryer basket and bake 6-8 mins until cooked through.
4. Divide shrimp into warmed pitas with feta, lettuce, tomato, olives and lemon squeeze.
5. Serve and enjoy!
6. **Variations & Ingredients Tips:**
7. Use cooked chicken instead of shrimp.
8. Add sliced red onion or cucumber to the pita filling.
9. Drizzle with tzatziki sauce instead of lemon juice.
10. **Per Serving:** Calories: 331; Total Fat: 14g; Saturated Fat: 4g; Cholesterol: 236mg; Sodium: 704mg; Total Carbs: 29g; Dietary Fiber: 4g; Total Sugars: 3g; Protein: 26g

British Fish & Chips

Servings: 4
Prep Time: 20 Minutes | Cooking Time: 40 Minutes
Ingredients:
- 2 peeled russet potatoes, thinly sliced
- 1 egg white
- 1 tbsp lemon juice
- 1/3 cup ground almonds
- 2 bread slices, crumbled
- 1/2 tsp dried basil
- 4 haddock fillets

Directions:
1. Preheat air fryer to 200°C/390°F.

2. Lay the potato slices in the frying basket and Air Fry for 11-15 minutes. Turn the fries a couple of times while cooking.
3. While the fries are cooking, whisk the egg white and lemon juice together in a bowl. On a plate, combine the almonds, breadcrumbs, and basil.
4. First, one at a time, dip the fillets into the egg mix and then coat in the almond/breadcrumb mix. Lay the fillets on a wire rack until the fries are done.
5. Preheat the oven to 175°C/350°F. After the fries are done, move them to a pan and place in the oven to keep warm.
6. Put the fish in the frying basket and Air Fry for 10-14 minutes or until cooked through, golden, and crispy.
7. Serve with the fries.
8. **Variations & Ingredients Tips:**
9. Use cod, pollock or halibut instead of haddock.
10. Season the fish batter with salt, pepper and Old Bay seasoning.
11. Serve with malt vinegar, tartar sauce and mushy peas.
12. **Per serving:** Calories: 400; Total Fat: 17g; Saturated Fat: 2g; Cholesterol: 80mg; Sodium: 260mg; Total Carbs: 34g; Dietary Fiber: 5g; Total Sugars: 2g; Protein: 31g

Korean-style Fried Calamari

Servings: 4
Prep Time: 15 Minutes | Cooking Time: 25 Minutes
Ingredients:
- 2 tbsp tomato paste
- 1 tbsp gochujang
- 1 tbsp lime juice
- 1 tsp lime zest
- 1 tsp smoked paprika
- 1/2 tsp salt
- 1 cup bread crumbs
- 150g calamari rings

Directions:
1. Preheat air fryer to 200°C/400°F.
2. Whisk tomato paste, gochujang, lime juice and zest, paprika, and salt in a bowl. In another bowl, add in the bread crumbs.
3. Dredge calamari rings in the tomato mixture, shake off excess, then roll through the crumbs.
4. Place calamari rings in the greased frying basket and Air Fry for 4-5 minutes, flipping once.
5. Serve.
6. **Variations & Ingredients Tips:**
7. Add some grated garlic or ginger to the tomato mixture.
8. Substitute gochujang with sriracha or sambal oelek.
9. Serve with a sweet chili dipping sauce or soy-ginger aioli.
10. **Per serving:** Calories: 180; Total Fat: 3g; Saturated Fat: 0.5g; Cholesterol: 265mg; Sodium: 860mg; Total Carbs: 25g; Dietary Fiber: 1g; Total Sugars: 3g; Protein: 14g

Creole Tilapia With Garlic Mayo

Servings: 4
Prep Time: 10 Minutes | Cooking Time: 20 Minutes
Ingredients:
- 4 tilapia fillets
- 2 tbsp olive oil
- 1 tsp paprika
- 1 tsp garlic powder
- 1 tsp dried basil
- 1/2 tsp Creole seasoning
- 1/2 tsp chili powder
- 2 garlic cloves, minced
- 1 tbsp mayonnaise
- 1 tsp olive oil
- 1/2 lemon, juiced

- Salt and pepper to taste

Directions:
1. Preheat air fryer to 200°C/400°F.
2. Coat the tilapia with some olive oil, then season with paprika, garlic powder, basil, and Creole seasoning.
3. Bake in the greased frying basket for 15 minutes, flipping once during cooking.
4. While the fish is cooking, whisk together garlic, mayonnaise, olive oil, lemon juice, chili powder, salt and pepper in a bowl.
5. Serve the cooked fish with the aioli.
6. **Variations & Ingredients Tips:**
7. Use catfish, cod or snapper instead of tilapia.
8. Add some diced tomatoes and green onions to the mayo for a remoulade.
9. Serve over a bed of dirty rice or Cajun-style coleslaw.
10. **Per serving:** Calories: 240; Total Fat: 13g; Saturated Fat: 2g; Cholesterol: 85mg; Sodium: 260mg; Total Carbs: 2g; Dietary Fiber: 0g; Total Sugars: 0g; Protein: 30g

Speedy Shrimp Paella

Servings: 4
Prep Time: 10 Minutes | Cooking Time: 20 Minutes
Ingredients:
- 2 cups cooked rice
- 1 red bell pepper, chopped
- 1/4 cup vegetable broth
- 1/2 tsp turmeric
- 1/2 tsp dried thyme
- 1 cup cooked small shrimp
- 1/2 cup baby peas
- 1 tomato, diced

Directions:
1. Preheat air fryer to 170°C/340°F.
2. Gently combine rice, bell pepper, broth, turmeric and thyme in a baking pan.
3. Bake in air fryer until rice is hot, about 9 minutes.
4. Remove pan, stir in shrimp, peas and tomato.
5. Return to air fryer and cook until bubbling and hot, 5-8 more minutes.
6. Serve and enjoy!
7. **Variations & Ingredients Tips:**
8. Use chicken or vegetable broth for more flavor.
9. Add sliced chorizo or bacon for a smoky flavor.
10. Stir in lemon juice or chopped parsley before serving.
11. **Per serving:** Calories: 180; Total Fat: 2g; Saturated Fat: 0g; Cholesterol: 35mg; Sodium: 120mg; Total Carbs: 32g; Dietary Fiber: 3g; Sugars: 4g; Protein: 9g

Vegetarian Recipes

Spicy Sesame Tempeh Slaw With Peanut Dressing

Servings: 2
Prep Time: 20 Minutes (plus Marinating Time) | Cooking Time: 8 Minutes

Ingredients:
- 2 cups hot water
- 1 teaspoon salt
- 227 grams tempeh, sliced into 2.5-cm-long pieces
- 2 tablespoons low-sodium soy sauce
- 2 tablespoons rice vinegar
- 1 tablespoon filtered water
- 2 teaspoons sesame oil
- ½ teaspoon fresh ginger

- 1 clove garlic, minced
- ¼ teaspoon black pepper
- ½ jalapeño, sliced
- 4 cups cabbage slaw
- 4 tablespoons Peanut Dressing (see the following recipe)
- 2 tablespoons fresh chopped cilantro
- 2 tablespoons chopped peanuts

Directions:
1. Mix the hot water with the salt and pour over the tempeh in a glass bowl. Stir and cover with a towel for 10 minutes.
2. Discard the water and leave the tempeh in the bowl.
3. In a medium bowl, mix the soy sauce, rice vinegar, filtered water, sesame oil, ginger, garlic, pepper, and jalapeño. Pour over the tempeh and cover with a towel. Place in the refrigerator to marinate for at least 2 hours.
4. Preheat the air fryer to 190°C/370°F. Remove the tempeh from the bowl and discard the remaining marinade.
5. Liberally spray the metal trivet that goes into the air fryer basket and place the tempeh on top of the trivet.
6. Cook for 4 minutes, flip, and cook another 4 minutes.
7. In a large bowl, mix the cabbage slaw with the Peanut Dressing and toss in the cilantro and chopped peanuts.
8. Portion onto 4 plates and place the cooked tempeh on top when cooking completes. Serve immediately.
9. **Variations & Ingredients Tips:**
10. Use extra-firm tofu instead of tempeh for a different protein.
11. Add shredded carrots, bell peppers, or edamame to the slaw.
12. Substitute peanut dressing with a sesame-ginger dressing.
13. **Per Serving:** Calories: 380; Total Fat: 23g; Saturated Fat: 3.5g; Sodium: 1210mg; Total Carbohydrates: 29g; Dietary Fiber: 8g; Total Sugars: 8g; Protein: 22g

Veggie Fried Rice

Servings: 4
Prep Time: 10 Minutes | Cooking Time: 25 Minutes
Ingredients:
- 1 cup cooked brown rice
- 1/3 cup chopped onion
- 1/2 cup chopped carrots
- 1/2 cup chopped bell peppers
- 1/2 cup chopped broccoli florets
- 3 tablespoons low-sodium soy sauce
- 1 tablespoon sesame oil
- 1 teaspoon ground ginger
- 1 teaspoon ground garlic powder
- 1/2 teaspoon black pepper
- 1/8 teaspoon salt
- 2 large eggs

Directions:
1. Preheat the air fryer to 190°C/370°F.
2. In a large bowl, mix together the brown rice, onions, carrots, bell pepper, and broccoli.
3. In a small bowl, whisk together the soy sauce, sesame oil, ginger, garlic powder, pepper, salt, and eggs.
4. Pour the egg mixture into the rice and vegetable mixture and mix together.
5. Liberally spray a 18-cm springform pan (or compatible air fryer dish) with olive oil. Add the rice mixture to the pan and cover with aluminum foil.
6. Place a metal trivet into the air fryer basket and set the pan on top. Cook for 15 minutes.
7. Carefully remove the pan from basket, discard the foil, and mix the rice. Return the rice to the air fryer basket, turning down the temperature to 180°C/350°F and cooking another 10 minutes.
8. Remove and let cool 5 minutes. Serve warm.

9. **Variations & Ingredients Tips:**
10. Add diced tofu or edamame for extra protein.
11. Use cauliflower rice for a low-carb option.
12. Drizzle with sriracha or chili garlic sauce for heat.
13. **Per Serving:** Calories: 253; Total Fat: 8g; Saturated Fat: 1g; Sodium: 553mg; Total Carbohydrates: 38g; Dietary Fiber: 5g; Total Sugars: 5g; Protein: 8g

Two-cheese Grilled Sandwiches

Servings: 2
Prep Time: 10 Minutes | Cooking Time: 30 Minutes
Ingredients:
- 4 sourdough bread slices
- 2 cheddar cheese slices
- 2 Swiss cheese slices
- 1 tbsp butter
- 2 dill pickles, sliced

Directions:
1. Preheat air fryer to 180°C/360°F.
2. Smear both sides of the sourdough bread with butter and place them in the air fryer basket. Toast the bread for 6 minutes, flipping once.
3. Divide the cheddar cheese between 2 of the bread slices. Cover the remaining 2 bread slices with Swiss cheese slices.
4. Bake for 10 more minutes until the cheeses have melted and lightly bubbled and the bread has golden brown.
5. Set the cheddar-covered bread slices on a serving plate, cover with pickles, and top each with the Swiss-covered slices.
6. Serve and enjoy!
7. **Variations & Ingredients Tips:**
8. Use different types of cheese like provolone, Gruyere, or Monterey Jack.

9. Add sliced tomatoes, avocado, or bacon for extra flavor and texture.
10. Serve with a side of mustard or mayonnaise for dipping.
11. **Per Serving:** Calories: 470; Total Fat: 29g; Saturated Fat: 17g; Sodium: 960mg; Total Carbohydrates: 34g; Dietary Fiber: 2g; Total Sugars: 2g; Protein: 22g

Tandoori Paneer Naan Pizza

Servings: 4
Prep Time: 15 Minutes | Cooking Time: 10 Minutes
Ingredients:
- 6 tablespoons plain Greek yogurt, divided
- 1 1/4 teaspoons garam masala, divided
- 1/2 teaspoon turmeric, divided
- 1/4 teaspoon garlic powder
- 1/2 teaspoon paprika, divided
- 1/2 teaspoon black pepper, divided
- 85g paneer, cut into small cubes
- 1 tablespoon extra-virgin olive oil
- 2 teaspoons minced garlic
- 4 cups baby spinach
- 2 tablespoons marinara sauce
- 1/4 teaspoon salt
- 2 plain naan breads (approximately 15cm in diameter)
- 1/2 cup shredded part-skim mozzarella cheese

Directions:
1. Preheat air fryer to 180°C/350°F.
2. Marinate paneer in 2 tbsp yogurt, 1/2 tsp garam masala, 1/4 tsp turmeric, garlic powder, 1/4 tsp paprika, 1/4 tsp pepper for 1 hour.

3. Sauté garlic in olive oil, then add spinach and remaining yogurt, marinara, spices and salt.
4. Divide spinach mixture between naans, top with marinated paneer.
5. Air fry one naan at a time for 4 mins. Top with 1/4 cup mozzarella and cook 4 more mins.
6. Repeat with second naan. Serve warm.
7. **Variations & Ingredients Tips:**
8. Use naan alternatives like pita or tortilla for the base.
9. Add sautéed onions, bell peppers or mushrooms to the topping.
10. Brush naans with garlic butter before baking.
11. **Per Serving:** Calories: 252; Total Fat: 11g; Saturated Fat: 4g; Sodium: 592mg; Total Carbohydrates: 28g; Dietary Fiber: 3g; Total Sugars: 5g; Protein: 12g

Roasted Veggie Bowls

Servings:4
Prep Time: 10 Minutes | Cooking Time: 30 Minutes
Ingredients:
- 1 cup Brussels sprouts, trimmed and quartered
- ½ onion, cut into half-moons
- ½ cup green beans, chopped
- 1 cup broccoli florets
- 1 red bell pepper, sliced
- 1 yellow bell pepper, sliced
- 1 tbsp olive oil
- ½ tsp chili powder
- ¼ tsp ground cumin
- ¼ tsp ground coriander

Directions:
1. Preheat air fryer to 180°C/350°F.

2. Combine all **ingredient**s in a bowl.
3. Place veggie mixture in the air fryer basket and Air Fry for 15 minutes, tossing every 5 minutes.
4. Divide between 4 medium bowls and serve.
5. **Variations & Ingredients Tips:**
6. Add sweet potato chunks or butternut squash for a heartier bowl.
7. Toss in canned chickpeas or black beans for added protein.
8. Drizzle with tahini sauce or balsamic glaze before serving.
9. **Per Serving:** Calories: 100; Total Fat: 5g; Saturated Fat: 0.5g; Sodium: 35mg; Total Carbohydrates: 12g; Dietary Fiber: 4g; Total Sugars: 5g; Protein: 3g

Veggie Burgers

Servings: 4
Prep Time: 10 Minutes | Cooking Time: 15 Minutes
Ingredients:
- 2 cans black beans, rinsed and drained
- 1/2 cup cooked quinoa
- 1/2 cup shredded raw sweet potato
- 1/4 cup diced red onion
- 2 teaspoons ground cumin
- 1 teaspoon coriander powder
- 1/2 teaspoon salt
- Oil for misting or cooking spray
- 8 slices bread
- Suggested toppings: lettuce, tomato, red onion, Pepper Jack cheese, guacamole

Directions:
1. In a medium bowl, mash the beans with a fork.
2. Add the quinoa, sweet potato, onion, cumin, coriander, and salt and mix well with the fork.

3. Shape into 4 patties, each 2-cm thick.
4. Mist both sides with oil or cooking spray and also mist the basket.
5. Cook at 200°C/390°F for 15 minutes.
6. Follow the recipe for Toast, Plain & Simple.
7. Pop the veggie burgers back in the air fryer for a minute or two to reheat if necessary.
8. Serve on the toast with your favorite burger toppings.
9. **Variations & Ingredients Tips:**
10. Use different beans like kidney or pinto.
11. Add breadcrumbs or oats for binding if needed.
12. Bake instead of air fry for a firmer patty.
13. **Per Serving:** Calories: 262; Total Fat: 3g; Saturated Fat: 0g; Sodium: 604mg; Total Carbohydrates: 48g; Dietary Fiber: 15g; Total Sugars: 4g; Protein: 14g

Pesto Pepperoni Pizza Bread

Servings:4
Prep Time: 10 Minutes | Cooking Time: 25 Minutes
Ingredients:
- 2 eggs, beaten
- 2 tbsp flour
- 2 tbsp cassava flour
- 1/3 cup whipping cream
- ¼ cup chopped pepperoni
- 1/3 cup grated mozzarella
- 2 tsp Italian seasoning
- ½ tsp baking powder
- ⅛ tsp salt
- 3 tsp grated Parmesan cheese
- ½ cup pesto

Directions:

1. Preheat air fryer to 150°C/300°F.
2. Combine all **ingredient**s, except for the Parmesan and pesto sauce, in a bowl until mixed.
3. Pour the batter into a 25-cm pizza pan. Place it in the air fryer basket and Bake for 20 minutes.
4. After, sprinkle Parmesan on top and cook for 1 minute.
5. Let chill for 5 minutes before slicing. Serve with warmed pesto sauce.
6. **Variations & Ingredients Tips:**
7. Use spinach or kale pesto for a greener taste and color.
8. Add sun-dried tomatoes or olives for a Mediterranean flair.
9. Sprinkle with red pepper flakes for some heat.
10. **Per Serving:** Calories: 320; Total Fat: 24g; Saturated Fat: 10g; Sodium: 510mg; Total Carbohydrates: 13g; Dietary Fiber: 1g; Total Sugars: 1g; Protein: 12g

Rigatoni With Roasted Onions, Fennel, Spinach And Lemon Pepper Ricotta

Servings: 2
Prep Time: 10 Minutes | Cooking Time: 13 Minutes
Ingredients:
- 1 red onion, rough chopped into large chunks
- 2 teaspoons olive oil, divided
- 1 bulb fennel, sliced 0.6-cm thick
- ¾ cup ricotta cheese
- 1½ teaspoons finely chopped lemon zest, plus more for garnish
- 1 teaspoon lemon juice
- salt and freshly ground black pepper
- 227 grams dried rigatoni pasta
- 3 cups baby spinach leaves

Directions:

1. Bring a large stockpot of salted water to a boil on the stovetop and Preheat the air fryer to 200°C/400°F.
2. While the water is coming to a boil, toss the chopped onion in 1 teaspoon of olive oil and transfer to the air fryer basket. Air-fry at 200°C/400°F for 5 minutes.
3. Toss the sliced fennel with 1 teaspoon of olive oil and add this to the air fryer basket with the onions. Continue to air-fry at 200°C/400°F for 8 minutes, shaking the basket a few times during the cooking process.
4. Combine the ricotta cheese, lemon zest and juice, ¼ teaspoon of salt and freshly ground black pepper in a bowl and stir until smooth.
5. Add the dried rigatoni to the boiling water and cook according to the package directions. When the pasta is cooked al dente, reserve one cup of the pasta water and drain the pasta into a colander.
6. Place the spinach in a serving bowl and immediately transfer the hot pasta to the bowl, wilting the spinach. Add the roasted onions and fennel and toss together. Add a little pasta water to the dish if it needs moistening. Then, dollop the lemon pepper ricotta cheese on top and nestle it into the hot pasta. Garnish with more lemon zest if desired.
7. **Variations & Ingredients Tips:**
8. Substitute fennel with sliced zucchini or eggplant.
9. Use goat cheese or feta instead of ricotta for a tangy flavor.
10. Add cooked chicken or shrimp for a non-vegetarian version.
11. **Per Serving:** Calories: 610; Total Fat: 19g; Saturated Fat: 9g; Sodium: 470mg; Total Carbohydrates: 89g; Dietary Fiber: 7g; Total Sugars: 8g; Protein: 24g

Meatless Kimchi Bowls

Servings:4
Prep Time: 10 Minutes | Cooking Time: 20 Minutes
Ingredients:
- 2 cups canned chickpeas

- 1 carrot, julienned
- 6 scallions, sliced
- 1 zucchini, diced
- 2 tbsp coconut aminos
- 2 tsp sesame oil
- 1 tsp rice vinegar
- 2 tsp granulated sugar
- 1 tbsp gochujang
- ¼ tsp salt
- ½ cup kimchi
- 2 tsp roasted sesame seeds

Directions:
1. Preheat air fryer to 180°C/350°F.
2. Combine all **ingredient**s, except for the kimchi, 2 scallions, and sesame seeds, in a baking pan.
3. Place the pan in the air fryer basket and Air Fry for 6 minutes.
4. Toss in kimchi and cook for 2 more minutes.
5. Divide between 2 bowls and garnish with the remaining scallions and sesame seeds.
6. Serve immediately.
7. **Variations & Ingredients Tips:**
8. Use tempeh or tofu instead of chickpeas for a different protein source.
9. Add sliced mushrooms or eggplant for meatier texture.
10. Adjust gochujang amount to make it spicier or milder.
11. **Per Serving:** Calories: 210; Total Fat: 6g; Saturated Fat: 1g; Sodium: 690mg; Total Carbohydrates: 31g; Dietary Fiber: 8g; Total Sugars: 8g; Protein: 10g

Caprese-style Sandwiches

Servings: 2

Prep Time: 10 Minutes | Cooking Time: 20 Minutes
Ingredients:
- 2 tbsp balsamic vinegar
- 4 sandwich bread slices
- 60 grams mozzarella shreds
- 3 tbsp pesto sauce
- 2 tomatoes, sliced
- 8 basil leaves
- 8 baby spinach leaves
- 2 tbsp olive oil

Directions:
1. Preheat air fryer at 175℃/350°F. Drizzle balsamic vinegar on the bottom of bread slices and smear with pesto sauce. Then, layer mozzarella cheese, tomatoes, baby spinach leaves and basil leaves on top. Add top bread slices. Rub the outside top and bottom of each sandwich with olive oil. Place them in the frying basket and Bake for 5 minutes, flipping once. Serve right away.
2. **Variations & Ingredients Tips:**
3. Use ciabatta, focaccia, or sourdough bread for a rustic sandwich.
4. Add sliced prosciutto or salami for a non-vegetarian version.
5. Drizzle with extra balsamic glaze or olive oil before serving for added flavor.
6. Per Serving (1 sandwich): Calories: 450; Cholesterol: 25mg; Total Fat: 28g; Saturated Fat: 7g; Sodium: 670mg; Total Carbohydrates: 37g; Dietary Fiber: 4g; Total Sugars: 8g; Protein: 16g

Vegetable Side Dishes Recipes

Toasted Choco-nuts

Servings: 2
Prep Time: 5 Minutes | Cooking Time: 10 Minutes
Ingredients:
- 2 cups almonds
- 2 teaspoons maple syrup
- 2 tablespoons cacao powder

Directions:
1. Preheat air fryer to 180°C/350°F.
2. Distribute the almonds in a single layer in the frying basket and Bake for 3 minutes.
3. Shake the basket and Bake for another 1 minute until golden brown.
4. Remove them to a bowl. Drizzle with maple syrup and toss.
5. Sprinkle with cacao powder and toss until well coated.
6. Let cool completely.
7. Store in a container at room temperature for up to 2 weeks or in the fridge for up to a month.
8. **Variations & Ingredients Tips:**
9. Use different types of nuts, such as cashews or pecans, for a variety of flavors and textures.
10. Add some ground cinnamon or vanilla extract for extra flavor.
11. For a savory version, replace the maple syrup and cacao powder with olive oil and your favorite spice blend.
12. **Per Serving:** Calories: 580; Total Fat: 51g; Saturated Fat: 4g; Cholesterol: 0mg; Sodium: 0mg; Total Carbs: 27g; Fiber: 13g; Sugars: 9g; Protein: 21g

Simple Baked Potatoes With Dill Yogurt

Servings: 4
Prep Time: 5 Minutes | Cooking Time: 45 Minutes
Ingredients:
- 4 Yukon gold potatoes
- Salt and black pepper
- Cooking oil spray
- 1/2 cup Greek yogurt
- 1/4 cup minced fresh dill

Directions:
1. Pierce potatoes several times with a fork. Lightly coat with cooking spray and season with salt.
2. Preheat air fryer to 205°C/400°F.
3. Place potatoes in greased air fryer basket.
4. Air fry for 30-35 minutes, flipping halfway, until potatoes are cooked through and slightly crispy.
5. Transfer baked potatoes to a serving dish.
6. Top each potato with a dollop of Greek yogurt and sprinkle with minced dill, salt and pepper.
7. **Variations & Ingredients Tips:**
8. Use russet or sweet potatoes instead of Yukon gold.
9. Add garlic, chives or bacon bits to the yogurt topping.
10. Brush potatoes with olive oil or melted butter before baking.
11. **Per Serving:** Calories: 165; Total Fat: 1g; Saturated Fat: 0g; Cholesterol: 2mg; Sodium: 106mg; Total Carbs: 34g; Dietary Fiber: 3g; Total Sugars: 3g; Protein: 6g

Citrusy Brussels Sprouts

Servings: 4
Prep Time: 10 Minutes | Cooking Time: 15 Minutes
Ingredients:
- 454g Brussels sprouts, quartered
- 1 clementine, cut into rings
- 2 garlic cloves, minced
- 1 tbsp olive oil
- 1 tbsp butter, melted
- ½ tsp salt

Directions:
1. Preheat air fryer to 182°C/360°F.
2. Add the quartered Brussels sprouts with the garlic, olive oil, butter and salt in a bowl and toss until well coated.
3. Pour the Brussels sprouts into the air fryer, top with the clementine slices.
4. Roast for 10 minutes.
5. Remove from the air fryer and set the clementines aside.
6. Toss the Brussels sprouts and serve.
7. **Variations & Ingredients Tips:**
8. Use orange or grapefruit sections instead of clementine.
9. Add sliced almonds or pecans for crunch.
10. Drizzle with balsamic glaze before serving.
11. **Per Serving:** Calories: 130; Total Fat: 8g; Saturated Fat: 2g; Cholesterol: 5mg; Sodium: 290mg; Total Carbs: 13g; Fiber: 5g; Sugars: 3g; Protein: 4g

Five-spice Roasted Sweet Potatoes

Servings: 4
Prep Time: 10 Minutes | Cooking Time: 12 Minutes
Ingredients:

- ½ teaspoon ground cinnamon
- ¼ teaspoon ground cumin
- ¼ teaspoon paprika
- 1 teaspoon chile powder
- ⅛ teaspoon turmeric
- ½ teaspoon salt (optional)
- Freshly ground black pepper
- 2 large sweet potatoes, peeled and cut into 2cm cubes (about 3 cups)
- 1 tablespoon olive oil

Directions:
1. In a large bowl, mix together cinnamon, cumin, paprika, chile powder, turmeric, salt, and pepper to taste.
2. Add potatoes and stir well.
3. Drizzle the seasoned potatoes with olive oil and stir until evenly coated.
4. Place seasoned potatoes in the air fryer baking pan or dish that fits basket.
5. Cook for 6 minutes at 198°C/390°F, stop and stir well.
6. Cook for an additional 6 minutes.
7. **Variations & Ingredients Tips:**
8. Add a pinch of cayenne for extra heat.
9. Toss with maple syrup before cooking.
10. Sprinkle with sliced green onions after roasting.
11. **Per Serving:** Calories: 150; Total Fat: 4g; Saturated Fat: 1g; Cholesterol: 0mg; Sodium: 200mg; Total Carbs: 26g; Fiber: 4g; Sugars: 7g; Protein: 2g

Patatas Bravas

Servings: 4
Prep Time: 10 Minutes | Cooking Time: 35 Minutes
Ingredients:

- 454g baby potatoes
- 1 onion, chopped
- 4 garlic cloves, minced
- 2 jalapeño peppers, minced
- 2 tsp olive oil
- 2 tsp ground chile de árbol
- 1/2 tsp ground cumin
- 1/2 tsp dried oregano

Directions:
1. Preheat air fryer to 190°C/370°F.
2. Put the potatoes, onion, garlic, jalapeños in a bowl and stir.
3. Pour in olive oil and stir again to coat.
4. Season with ground chile de árbol, cumin, and oregano.
5. Put the bowl in the air fryer basket and air fry for 22-28 minutes, shaking once.
6. Serve hot.
7. **Variations & Ingredients Tips:**
8. Use a blend of chili powders like ancho and chipotle.
9. Add chopped chorizo or bacon.
10. Drizzle with garlic aioli or sour cream before serving.
11. **Per serving:** Calories: 112; Total Fat: 3g; Saturated Fat: 0g; Cholesterol: 0mg; Sodium: 36mg; Total Carbohydrates: 20g; Dietary Fiber: 3g; Total Sugars: 2g; Protein: 3g

Onion Rings

Servings: 4
Prep Time: 10 Minutes | Cooking Time: 12 Minutes
Ingredients:
- 1 large (227g) onion
- 1/2 cup + 2 tbsp flour
- 1/2 teaspoon salt
- 1/2 cup + 2 tbsp beer

- 1 cup crushed panko breadcrumbs
- Oil for misting or cooking spray

Directions:
1. Peel onion, slice into rings and separate into rings.
2. In a bowl, mix flour and salt. Add beer and stir into a thick batter.
3. Coat onion rings in the batter.
4. Place breadcrumbs in a bag or container.
5. Remove rings from batter, shake off excess, then coat in breadcrumbs.
6. Arrange breaded rings on a tray. Mist with oil spray.
7. Place rings in air fryer basket in a single layer.
8. Cook at 200°C/390°F for 5 minutes. Shake, mist with oil, and cook 5 more minutes.
9. Shake, mist again and cook 2 more minutes until crispy.
10. **Variations & Ingredients Tips:**
11. Use beer batter mix instead of making your own batter.
12. Add cajun seasoning or ranch powder to the breading.
13. Serve with ranch, barbecue sauce or chipotle mayo.
14. **Per serving:** Calories: 220; Total Fat: 3g; Saturated Fat: 0g; Cholesterol: 0mg; Sodium: 420mg; Total Carbohydrates: 42g; Dietary Fiber: 3g; Total Sugars: 4g; Protein: 6g

Tasty Brussels Sprouts With Guanciale

Servings: 4
Prep Time: 10 Minutes | Cooking Time: 50 Minutes
Ingredients:
- 3 guanciale slices, halved
- 450 g Brussels sprouts, halved
- 2 tablespoons olive oil
- ¼ teaspoon salt
- ¼ teaspoon dried thyme

Directions:
1. Preheat air fryer to 180°C/350°F.
2. Lay the guanciale in the air fryer, until crispy, 10 minutes. Remove and drain on a paper towel. Give the guanciale a rough chop and set aside.
3. Coat Brussels sprouts with olive oil in a large bowl. Add salt and thyme, then toss.
4. Place the sprouts in the frying basket. Air Fry for about 12-15 minutes, shake the basket once until the sprouts are golden and tender.
5. Top with guanciale and serve.
6. **Variations & Ingredients Tips:**
7. Use bacon or pancetta instead of guanciale for a different flavor profile.
8. Add some minced garlic or red pepper flakes to the Brussels sprouts for extra flavor.
9. Serve the Brussels sprouts with a dipping sauce, such as honey mustard or balsamic glaze.
10. **Per Serving:** Calories: 160; Total Fat: 12g; Saturated Fat: 3.5g; Cholesterol: 15mg; Sodium: 320mg; Total Carbs: 8g; Fiber: 3g; Sugars: 2g; Protein: 6g

Steak Fries

Servings: 4
Prep Time: 5 Minutes | Cooking Time: 25 Minutes
Ingredients:
- 900 g Medium Yukon Gold or other yellow potatoes (peeled or not—your choice)
- 2 tablespoons olive oil
- ½ teaspoon, or more to taste table salt
- ½ teaspoon, or more to taste ground black pepper

Directions:
1. Preheat the air fryer to 180°C/350°F.
2. Cut the potatoes lengthwise into wedges about 5 cm wide at the outer edge. Toss these wedges in a bowl with the oil, salt, and pepper until the wedges are evenly coated in the oil. (Start with the minimum amounts of salt and pepper we recommend—you can always add more later.)
3. When the machine is at temperature, set the wedges in the basket in a crisscross stack, with about half of the wedges first lining in the basket's bottom, then others set on top of those at a 45-degree angle. Air-fry undisturbed for 15 minutes.
4. Increase the machine's temperature to 200°C/400°F. Toss the fries so they're no longer in a crisscross pattern but more like a mound. Air-fry for 10 minutes more (from the moment you raise the temperature), tossing and rearranging the fries once, until they're crisp and brown.
5. Pour them onto a wire rack and cool for a few minutes before serving hot.
6. **Variations & Ingredients Tips:**
7. Try using sweet potatoes or russet potatoes for a different flavor and texture.
8. Season the fries with garlic powder, onion powder, paprika, or your favorite spice blend before cooking.
9. Serve the fries with ketchup, mayo, or your favorite dipping sauce.
10. **Per Serving:** Calories: 230; Total Fat: 7g; Saturated Fat: 1g; Cholesterol: 0mg; Sodium: 300mg; Total Carbs: 38g; Fiber: 4g; Sugars: 1g; Protein: 4g

Buttered Brussels Sprouts

Servings: 4
Prep Time: 5 Minutes | Cooking Time: 30 Minutes
Ingredients:
- ¼ cup grated Parmesan

- 2 tbsp butter, melted
- 455g Brussels sprouts
- Salt and pepper to taste

Directions:
1. Preheat air fryer to 165°C/330°F.
2. Trim the bottoms of the sprouts and remove any discolored leaves.
3. Place the sprouts in a medium bowl along with butter, salt and pepper. Toss to coat, then place them in the frying basket.
4. Roast for 20 minutes, shaking the basket twice. When done, the sprouts should be crisp with golden-brown color.
5. Plate the sprouts in a serving dish and toss with Parmesan cheese.
6. **Variations & Ingredients Tips:**
7. Add crushed garlic or garlic powder to the butter mixture.
8. Toss with balsamic glaze or lemon juice after cooking.
9. Use olive oil instead of butter to make it vegan.
10. **Per Serving:** Calories: 130; Total Fat: 8g; Saturated Fat: 4g; Cholesterol: 15mg; Sodium: 230mg; Total Carbs: 11g; Fiber: 4g; Sugars: 3g; Protein: 6g

Green Peas With Mint

Servings: 4
Prep Time: 5 Minutes | Cooking Time: 5 Minutes
Ingredients:
- 1 cup shredded lettuce
- 284g package frozen green peas, thawed
- 1 tablespoon fresh mint, shredded
- 1 teaspoon melted butter

Directions:

1. Lay the shredded lettuce in the air fryer basket.
2. Toss together the peas, mint, and melted butter and spoon over the lettuce.
3. Cook at 180°C/360°F for 5 minutes, until peas are warm and lettuce wilts.
4. **Variations & Ingredients Tips:**
5. Add lemon zest or juice for extra brightness.
6. Use olive oil instead of butter.
7. Mix in crumbled feta or goat cheese.
8. **Per serving:** Calories: 80; Total Fat: 1.5g; Saturated Fat: 0.5g; Cholesterol: 0mg; Sodium: 65mg; Total Carbohydrates: 12g; Dietary Fiber: 4g; Total Sugars: 5g; Protein: 5g

Sandwiches And Burgers Recipes

Dijon Thyme Burgers

Servings: 3
Prep Time: 15 Minutes | Cooking Time: 18 Minutes
Ingredients:
- 450 grams lean ground beef
- ⅓ cup panko breadcrumbs
- ¼ cup finely chopped onion
- 3 tablespoons Dijon mustard
- 1 tablespoon chopped fresh thyme
- 4 teaspoons Worcestershire sauce
- 1 teaspoon salt
- freshly ground black pepper
- Topping (optional):
- 2 tablespoons Dijon mustard
- 1 tablespoon dark brown sugar

- 1 teaspoon Worcestershire sauce
- 115 grams sliced Swiss cheese, optional

Directions:
1. Combine all the burger **ingredient**s together in a large bowl and mix well. Divide the meat into 4 equal portions and then form the burgers, being careful not to over-handle the meat. One good way to do this is to throw the meat back and forth from one hand to another, packing the meat each time you catch it. Flatten the balls into patties, making an indentation in the center of each patty with your thumb (this will help it stay flat as it cooks) and flattening the sides of the burgers so that they will fit nicely into the air fryer basket.
2. Preheat the air fryer to 190℃/370°F.
3. If you don't have room for all four burgers, air-fry two or three burgers at a time for 8 minutes. Flip the burgers over and air-fry for another 6 minutes.
4. While the burgers are cooking combine the Dijon mustard, dark brown sugar, and Worcestershire sauce in a small bowl and mix well. This optional topping to the burgers really adds a boost of flavor at the end. Spread the Dijon topping evenly on each burger. If you cooked the burgers in batches, return the first batch to the cooker at this time – it's ok to place the fourth burger on top of the others in the center of the basket. Air-fry the burgers for another 3 minutes.
5. Finally, if desired, top each burger with a slice of Swiss cheese. Lower the air fryer temperature to 165℃/330°F and air-fry for another minute to melt the cheese. Serve the burgers on toasted brioche buns, dressed the way you like them.
6. **Variations & Ingredients Tips:**
7. Use ground turkey or chicken for a leaner burger option.
8. Add minced garlic or finely chopped herbs like parsley or chives for extra flavor.
9. Substitute panko breadcrumbs with regular breadcrumbs or oats for a different texture.
10. Per Serving (1 burger with cheese): Calories: 500; Cholesterol: 120mg; Total Fat: 27g; Saturated Fat: 11g;

Sodium: 1180mg; Total Carbohydrates: 21g; Dietary Fiber: 1g; Total Sugars: 5g; Protein: 41g

Provolone Stuffed Meatballs

Servings: 4
Prep Time: 20 Minutes | Cooking Time: 12 Minutes
Ingredients:
- 1 tablespoon olive oil
- 1 small onion, very finely chopped
- 1 to 2 cloves garlic, minced
- 340 grams ground beef
- 340 grams ground pork
- ¾ cup breadcrumbs
- ¼ cup grated Parmesan cheese
- ¼ cup finely chopped fresh parsley (or 1 tablespoon dried parsley)
- ½ teaspoon dried oregano
- 1½ teaspoons salt
- freshly ground black pepper
- 2 eggs, lightly beaten
- 140 grams sharp or aged provolone cheese, cut into 2.5-cm cubes

Directions:
1. Preheat a skillet over medium-high heat. Add the oil and cook the onion and garlic until tender, but not browned.
2. Transfer the onion and garlic to a large bowl and add the beef, pork, breadcrumbs, Parmesan cheese, parsley, oregano, salt, pepper and eggs. Mix well until all the **ingredient**s are combined. Divide the mixture into 12 evenly sized balls. Make one meatball at a time, by pressing a hole in the meatball mixture with your finger and pushing a piece of

provolone cheese into the hole. Mold the meat back into a ball, enclosing the cheese.
3. Preheat the air fryer to 190°C/380°F.
4. Working in two batches, transfer six of the meatballs to the air fryer basket and air-fry for 12 minutes, shaking the basket and turning the meatballs a couple of times during the cooking process. Repeat with the remaining six meatballs. You can pop the first batch of meatballs into the air fryer for the last two minutes of cooking to re-heat them. Serve warm.
5. **Variations & Ingredients Tips:**
6. Substitute beef and pork with ground turkey or chicken for a leaner meatball option.
7. Use mozzarella or fontina cheese instead of provolone for a milder flavor.
8. Serve meatballs with marinara sauce, in sub rolls, or over pasta for a complete meal.
9. Per Serving (3 meatballs): Calories: 520; Cholesterol: 180mg; Total Fat: 36g; Saturated Fat: 15g; Sodium: 1160mg; Total Carbohydrates: 18g; Dietary Fiber: 1g; Total Sugars: 2g; Protein: 35g

Chicken Gyros

Servings: 4
Prep Time: 10 Minutes (plus Marinating Time) | Cooking Time: 14 Minutes
Ingredients:
- 4 110to 140-gram boneless skinless chicken thighs, trimmed of any fat blobs
- 2 tablespoons Lemon juice
- 2 tablespoons Red wine vinegar
- 2 tablespoons Olive oil
- 2 teaspoons Dried oregano
- 2 teaspoons Minced garlic
- 1 teaspoon Table salt

- 1 teaspoon Ground black pepper
- 4 Pita pockets (gluten-free, if a concern)
- ½ cup Chopped tomatoes
- ½ cup Bottled regular, low-fat, or fat-free ranch dressing (gluten-free, if a concern)

Directions:
1. Mix the thighs, lemon juice, vinegar, oil, oregano, garlic, salt, and pepper in a zip-closed bag. Seal, gently massage the marinade into the meat through the plastic, and refrigerate for at least 2 hours or up to 6 hours. (Longer than that and the meat can turn rubbery.)
2. Set the plastic bag out on the counter (to make the contents a little less frigid). Preheat the air fryer to 190℃/375°F.
3. When the machine is at temperature, use kitchen tongs to place the thighs in the basket in one layer. Discard the marinade. Air-fry the chicken thighs undisturbed for 12 minutes, or until browned and an instant-read meat thermometer inserted into the thickest part of one thigh registers 75℃/165°F. You may need to air-fry the chicken 2 minutes longer if the machine's temperature is 70℃/360°F.
4. Use kitchen tongs to transfer the thighs to a cutting board. Cool for 5 minutes, then set one thigh in each of the pita pockets. Top each with 2 tablespoons chopped tomatoes and 2 tablespoons dressing. Serve warm.
5. **Variations & Ingredients Tips:**
6. Substitute chicken thighs with chicken breast for a leaner option.
7. Add shredded lettuce, sliced onions, or cucumbers for extra crunch and flavor.
8. Use homemade tzatziki sauce instead of ranch dressing for a more authentic taste.
9. **Per Serving:** Calories: 460; Cholesterol: 95mg; Total Fat: 28g; Saturated Fat: 5g; Sodium: 1070mg; Total Carbohydrates: 29g; Dietary Fiber: 2g; Total Sugars: 4g; Protein: 25g

Perfect Burgers

Servings: 3
Prep Time: 10 Minutes | Cooking Time: 13 Minutes
Ingredients:
- 510 grams 90% lean ground beef
- 1½ tablespoons Worcestershire sauce (gluten-free, if a concern)
- ½ teaspoon Ground black pepper
- 3 Hamburger buns (gluten-free if a concern), split open

Directions:
1. Preheat the air fryer to 190℃/375°F.
2. Gently mix the ground beef, Worcestershire sauce, and pepper in a bowl until well combined but preserving as much of the meat's fibers as possible. Divide this mixture into two 15-cm patties for the small batch, three 12.5-cm patties for the medium, or four 12.5-cm patties for the large. Make a thumbprint indentation in the center of each patty, about halfway through the meat.
3. Set the patties in the basket in one layer with some space between them. Air-fry undisturbed for 10 minutes, or until an instant-read meat thermometer inserted into the center of a burger registers 70℃/160°F (a medium-well burger). You may need to add 2 minutes cooking time if the air fryer is at 180℃/360°F.
4. Use a nonstick-safe spatula, and perhaps a flatware fork for balance, to transfer the burgers to a cutting board. Set the buns cut side down in the basket in one layer (working in batches as necessary) and air-fry undisturbed for 1 minute, to toast a bit and warm up. Serve the burgers in the warm buns.
5. **Variations & Ingredients Tips:**
6. Mix in finely chopped onions, garlic, or herbs to the burger mixture for extra flavor.

7. Use a mixture of ground beef and ground pork or lamb for a juicier, more flavorful burger.
8. Top burgers with your favorite cheese, bacon, avocado, or sautéed mushrooms.
9. Per Serving (1 burger): Calories: 420; Cholesterol: 105mg; Total Fat: 22g; Saturated Fat: 8g; Sodium: 460mg; Total Carbohydrates: 23g; Dietary Fiber: 1g; Total Sugars: 3g; Protein: 34g

Chili Cheese Dogs

Servings: 3
Prep Time: 10 Minutes | Cooking Time: 12 Minutes

Ingredients:
- 340 grams Lean ground beef
- 1½ tablespoons Chile powder
- 240 grams plus 2 tablespoons Jarred sofrito
- 3 Hot dogs (gluten-free, if a concern)
- 3 Hot dog buns (gluten-free, if a concern), split open lengthwise
- 3 tablespoons Finely chopped scallion
- 60 grams Shredded Cheddar cheese

Directions:
1. Crumble the ground beef into a medium or large saucepan set over medium heat. Brown well, stirring often to break up the clumps. Add the chile powder and cook for 30 seconds, stirring the whole time. Stir in the sofrito and bring to a simmer. Reduce the heat to low and simmer, stirring occasionally, for 5 minutes. Keep warm.
2. Preheat the air fryer to 200℃/400°F.
3. When the machine is at temperature, put the hot dogs in the basket and air-fry undisturbed for 10 minutes, or until the hot dogs are bubbling and blistered, even a little crisp.

4. Use kitchen tongs to put the hot dogs in the buns. Top each with about 120 grams of the ground beef mixture, 1 tablespoon of the minced scallion, and 20 grams of the cheese. (The scallion should go under the cheese so it superheats and wilts a bit.) Set the filled hot dog buns in the basket and air-fry undisturbed for 2 minutes, or until the cheese has melted.
5. Remove the basket from the machine. Cool the chili cheese dogs in the basket for 5 minutes before serving.
6. **Variations & Ingredients Tips:**
7. Use turkey or veggie hot dogs for a healthier option.
8. Substitute cheddar cheese with your favorite melty cheese, such as pepper jack or Swiss.
9. Add diced onions or jalapeños to the chili for extra flavor and heat.
10. **Per Serving:** Calories: 580; Cholesterol: 110mg; Total Fat: 32g; Saturated Fat: 13g; Sodium: 1420mg; Total Carbohydrates: 36g; Dietary Fiber: 5g; Total Sugars: 6g; Protein: 38g

Black Bean Veggie Burgers

Servings: 3
Prep Time: 15 Minutes | Cooking Time: 10 Minutes
Ingredients:
- 1 cup Drained and rinsed canned black beans
- ⅓ cup Pecan pieces
- ⅓ cup Rolled oats (not quick-cooking or steel-cut; gluten-free, if a concern)
- 2 tablespoons (or 1 small egg) Pasteurized egg substitute, such as Egg Beaters (gluten-free, if a concern)
- 2 teaspoons Red ketchup-like chili sauce, such as Heinz
- ¼ teaspoon Ground cumin
- ¼ teaspoon Dried oregano
- ¼ teaspoon Table salt

- ¼ teaspoon Ground black pepper
- Olive oil
- Olive oil spray

Directions:
1. Preheat the air fryer to 200°C/400°F.
2. Put the beans, pecans, oats, egg substitute or egg, chili sauce, cumin, oregano, salt, and pepper in a food processor. Cover and process to a coarse paste that will hold its shape like sugar-cookie dough, adding olive oil in 1-teaspoon increments to get the mixture to blend smoothly. The amount of olive oil is actually dependent on the internal moisture content of the beans and the oats. Figure on about 1 tablespoon (three 1-teaspoon additions) for the smaller batch, with proportional increases for the other batches. A little too much olive oil can't hurt, but a dry paste will fall apart as it cooks and a far-too-wet paste will stick to the basket.
3. Scrape down and remove the blade. Using clean, wet hands, form the paste into two 10 cm patties for the small batch, three 10 cm patties for the medium, or four 10 cm patties for the large batch, setting them one by one on a cutting board. Generously coat both sides of the patties with olive oil spray.
4. Set them in the basket in one layer. Air-fry undisturbed for 10 minutes, or until lightly browned and crisp at the edges.
5. Use a nonstick-safe spatula, and perhaps a flatware fork for balance, to transfer the burgers to a wire rack. Cool for 5 minutes before serving.
6. **Variations & Ingredients Tips:**
7. Add finely chopped vegetables like bell peppers, onions, or carrots for extra flavor and nutrition.
8. Experiment with different spices and herbs, such as smoked paprika, garlic powder, or cilantro.
9. For a gluten-free version, ensure all **ingredient**s are certified gluten-free.
10. **Per Serving:** Calories: 280; Cholesterol: 0mg; Total Fat: 15g; Saturated Fat: 2g; Sodium: 420mg; Total Carbohydrates: 28g; Dietary Fiber: 8g; Total Sugars: 2g; Protein: 10g

Reuben Sandwiches

Servings: 2
Prep Time: 10 Minutes | Cooking Time: 11 Minutes
Ingredients:
- 225 grams Sliced deli corned beef
- 4 teaspoons Regular or low-fat mayonnaise (not fat-free)
- 4 Rye bread slices
- 2 tablespoons plus 2 teaspoons Russian dressing
- ½ cup Purchased sauerkraut, squeezed by the handful over the sink to get rid of excess moisture
- 55 grams (2 to 4 slices) Swiss cheese slices (optional)

Directions:
1. Set the corned beef in the basket, slip the basket into the machine, and heat the air fryer to 200℃/400°F. Air-fry undisturbed for 3 minutes from the time the basket is put in the machine, just to warm up the meat.
2. Use kitchen tongs to transfer the corned beef to a cutting board. Spread 1 teaspoon mayonnaise on one side of each slice of rye bread, rubbing the mayonnaise into the bread with a small flatware knife.
3. Place the bread slices mayonnaise side down on a cutting board. Spread the Russian dressing over the "dry" side of each slice. For one sandwich, top one slice of bread with the corned beef, sauerkraut, and cheese (if using). For two sandwiches, top two slices of bread each with half of the corned beef, sauerkraut, and cheese (if using). Close the sandwiches with the remaining bread, setting it mayonnaise side up on top.
4. Set the sandwich(es) in the basket and air-fry undisturbed for 8 minutes, or until browned and crunchy.
5. Use a nonstick-safe spatula, and perhaps a flatware fork for balance, to transfer the sandwich(es) to a cutting board. Cool for 2 or 3 minutes before slicing in half and serving.

6. **Variations & Ingredients Tips:**
7. Substitute corned beef with pastrami for a classic New York deli taste.
8. Use Thousand Island dressing instead of Russian dressing for a tangy, sweet flavor.
9. Add sliced dill pickles or mustard to the sandwich for extra zing.
10. Per Serving (1 sandwich): Calories: 520; Cholesterol: 75mg; Total Fat: 30g; Saturated Fat: 9g; Sodium: 2020mg; Total Carbohydrates: 36g; Dietary Fiber: 4g; Total Sugars: 6g; Protein: 29g

Eggplant Parmesan Subs

Servings: 2
Prep Time: 10 Minutes | Cooking Time: 13 Minutes
Ingredients:
- 4 Peeled eggplant slices (about 1.25 cm thick and 7.5 cm in diameter)
- Olive oil spray
- 2 tablespoons plus 2 teaspoons Jarred pizza sauce, any variety except creamy
- ¼ cup (about 20 grams) Finely grated Parmesan cheese
- 2 Small, long soft rolls, such as hero, hoagie, or Italian sub rolls (gluten-free, if a concern), split open lengthwise

Directions:
1. Preheat the air fryer to 175℃/350°F.
2. When the machine is at temperature, coat both sides of the eggplant slices with olive oil spray. Set them in the basket in one layer and air-fry undisturbed for 10 minutes, until lightly browned and softened.
3. Increase the machine's temperature to 190℃/375°F (or 185℃/370°F, if that's the closest setting—unless the machine

is already at 180℃/360°F, in which case leave it alone). Top each eggplant slice with 2 teaspoons pizza sauce, then 1 tablespoon of cheese. Air-fry undisturbed for 2 minutes, or until the cheese has melted.
4. Use a nonstick-safe spatula, and perhaps a flatware fork for balance, to transfer the eggplant slices cheese side up to a cutting board. Set the roll(s) cut side down in the basket in one layer (working in batches as necessary) and air-fry undisturbed for 1 minute, to toast the rolls a bit and warm them up. Set 2 eggplant slices in each warm roll.
5. **Variations & Ingredients Tips:**
6. Use zucchini slices instead of eggplant for a different vegetable option.
7. Add a slice of fresh mozzarella on top of the Parmesan for extra cheesiness.
8. Sprinkle some dried herbs like oregano or basil on the eggplant before cooking for extra flavor.
9. Per Serving (1 sandwich): Calories: 280; Cholesterol: 10mg; Total Fat: 9g; Saturated Fat: 3g; Sodium: 840mg; Total Carbohydrates: 40g; Dietary Fiber: 5g; Total Sugars: 8g; Protein: 11g

Inside Out Cheeseburgers

Servings: 2
Prep Time: 15 Minutes | Cooking Time: 20 Minutes
Ingredients:
- 340 grams lean ground beef
- 3 tablespoons minced onion
- 4 teaspoons ketchup
- 2 teaspoons yellow mustard
- salt and freshly ground black pepper
- 4 slices of Cheddar cheese, broken into smaller pieces
- 8 hamburger dill pickle chips

Directions:
1. Combine the ground beef, minced onion, ketchup, mustard, salt and pepper in a large bowl. Mix well to thoroughly combine the **ingredient**s. Divide the meat into four equal portions.
2. To make the stuffed burgers, flatten each portion of meat into a thin patty. Place 4 pickle chips and half of the cheese onto the center of two of the patties, leaving a rim around the edge of the patty exposed. Place the remaining two patties on top of the first and press the meat together firmly, sealing the edges tightly. With the burgers on a flat surface, press the sides of the burger with the palm of your hand to create a straight edge. This will help keep the stuffing inside the burger while it cooks.
3. Preheat the air fryer to 190 ℃/370°F.
4. Place the burgers inside the air fryer basket and air-fry for 20 minutes, flipping the burgers over halfway through the cooking time.
5. Serve the cheeseburgers on buns with lettuce and tomato.
6. **Variations & Ingredients Tips:**
7. Use different types of cheese like Swiss, pepper jack, or blue cheese for a unique flavor.
8. Add crispy bacon pieces or sautéed mushrooms to the stuffing for extra richness.
9. Brush the burgers with a mixture of melted butter and minced garlic before cooking for added flavor.
10. Per Serving (1 burger): Calories: 510; Cholesterol: 145mg; Total Fat: 32g; Saturated Fat: 14g; Sodium: 780mg; Total Carbohydrates: 12g; Dietary Fiber: 1g; Total Sugars: 6g; Protein: 42g

Asian Glazed Meatballs

Servings: 4

Prep Time: 15 Minutes | Cooking Time: 10 Minutes
Ingredients:
- 1 large shallot, finely chopped
- 2 cloves garlic, minced
- 1 tablespoon grated fresh ginger
- 2 teaspoons fresh thyme, finely chopped
- 1½ cups brown mushrooms, very finely chopped (a food processor works well here)
- 2 tablespoons soy sauce
- freshly ground black pepper
- ½ kg ground beef
- ¼ kg ground pork
- 3 egg yolks
- 1 cup Thai sweet chili sauce (spring roll sauce)
- ¼ cup toasted sesame seeds
- 2 scallions, sliced

Directions:
1. Combine the shallot, garlic, ginger, thyme, mushrooms, soy sauce, freshly ground black pepper, ground beef and pork, and egg yolks in a bowl and mix the **ingredient**s together. Gently shape the mixture into 24 balls, about the size of a golf ball.
2. Preheat the air fryer to 190℃/380°F.
3. Working in batches, air-fry the meatballs for 8 minutes, turning the meatballs over halfway through the cooking time. Drizzle some of the Thai sweet chili sauce on top of each meatball and return the basket to the air fryer, air-frying for another 2 minutes. Reserve the remaining Thai sweet chili sauce for serving.
4. As soon as the meatballs are done, sprinkle with toasted sesame seeds and transfer them to a serving platter. Scatter the scallions around and serve warm.
5. **Variations & Ingredients Tips:**
6. Use a food processor to finely chop the mushrooms for better texture in the meatballs.
7. Work in batches when air frying the meatballs to ensure even cooking and browning.

8. Drizzle the Thai sweet chili sauce over the meatballs towards the end of cooking for a nice glaze.
9. **Per Serving:** Calories: 550; Cholesterol: 205mg; Total Fat: 32g; Saturated Fat: 11g; Sodium: 1300mg; Total Carbohydrates: 36g; Dietary Fiber: 2g; Total Sugars: 23g; Protein: 29g

Desserts And Sweets

Strawberry Donuts

Servings: 4
Prep Time: 25 Minutes | Cooking Time: 55 Minutes
Ingredients:
- 3/4 cup Greek yogurt
- 2 tbsp maple syrup
- 1 tbsp vanilla extract
- 2 tsp active dry yeast
- 1 1/2 cups all-purpose flour
- 3 tbsp milk
- 1/2 cup strawberry jam

Directions:
1. Preheat air fryer to 175°C/350°F.
2. Whisk the Greek yogurt, maple syrup, vanilla extract, and yeast until well combined. Then toss in flour until you get a sticky dough.
3. Let rest covered for 10 minutes. Flour a parchment paper on a flat surface, lay the dough, sprinkle with some flour, and flatten to 1.3cm thick with a rolling pin.
4. Using a 8cm cookie cutter, cut the donuts. Repeat the process until no dough is left.

5. Place the donuts in the basket and let rise for 15-20 minutes. Spread some milk on top of each donut and Air Fry for 4 minutes. Turn the donuts, spread more milk, and Air Fry for 4 more minutes until golden brown.
6. Let cool for 15 minutes. Using a knife, cut the donuts 3/4 lengthwise, brush 1 tbsp of strawberry jam on each and close them. Serve.
7. **Variations & Ingredients Tips:**
8. Use other jam flavors like blueberry or raspberry.
9. Coat in cinnamon-sugar after baking.
10. Fill with cream cheese frosting.
11. **Per serving:** Calories: 320; Total Fat: 3g; Saturated Fat: 1g; Cholesterol: 5mg; Sodium: 100mg; Total Carbs: 62g; Dietary Fiber: 2g; Total Sugars: 20g; Protein: 8g

Strawberry Pastry Rolls

Servings: 4
Prep Time: 20 Minutes | Cooking Time: 6 Minutes
Ingredients:
- 85-g low-fat cream cheese
- 2 tablespoons plain yogurt
- 2 teaspoons sugar
- 1/4 teaspoon pure vanilla extract
- 225-g fresh strawberries
- 8 sheets phyllo dough
- Butter-flavored cooking spray
- 1/4–1/2 cup dark chocolate chips (optional)

Directions:
1. In a bowl, combine cream cheese, yogurt, sugar, vanilla. Beat until smooth, 1 min.
2. Wash berries, destem. Chop enough for 1/2 cup. Stir into cheese mix.

3. Preheat air fryer to 165°C/330°F.
4. Cover phyllo sheets with waxed paper and damp towel. Remove 1 at a time as using.
5. For 1 roll: Lay 1 sheet phyllo, spray with butter spray, top with 2nd sheet, spray again.
6. Place 1/4 filling (3 tbsp) 1.3cm from short edge. Fold over filling, roll up, folding in sides. Spray outside with butter spray.
7. Place 4 rolls in basket, seam-down, spaced apart. Cook at 165°C/330°F for 6 mins until golden.
8. Repeat with remaining rolls.
9. Let cool. Slice remaining berries. Melt chocolate if using.
10. Top pastries with berries, drizzle with chocolate.
11. **Variations & Ingredients Tips:**
12. Use other fresh berries.
13. Dust with powdered sugar instead of chocolate.
14. Stuff with cream cheese or nutella filling.
15. **Per serving:** Calories: 185; Total Fat: 8g; Saturated Fat: 4g; Cholesterol: 15mg; Sodium: 130mg; Total Carbs: 25g; Dietary Fiber: 2g; Total Sugars: 9g; Protein: 5g

Oatmeal Blackberry Crisp

Servings: 6
Prep Time: 10 Minutes | Cooking Time: 20 Minutes
Ingredients:
- 1 cup rolled oats
- 1/2 cup flour
- 1/4 cup olive oil
- 1/4 tsp salt
- 1 tsp cinnamon
- 1/3 cup honey
- 4 cups blackberries

Directions:
1. Preheat air fryer to 180°C/350°F.
2. Combine rolled oats, flour, olive oil, salt, cinnamon, and honey in a large bowl. Mix well.
3. Spread blackberries on the bottom of a greased cooking pan. Cover them with the oat mixture.
4. Place pan in air fryer and Bake for 15 minutes.
5. Cool for a few minutes. Serve and enjoy.
6. **Variations & Ingredients Tips:**
7. Substitute other fresh or frozen berries for the blackberries.
8. Add 1/2 cup chopped nuts like pecans or walnuts to the oat topping.
9. Use whole wheat flour for more fiber.
10. **Per serving:** Calories: 335; Total Fat: 13g; Saturated Fat: 2g; Cholesterol: 0mg; Sodium: 85mg; Total Carbs: 52g; Dietary Fiber: 7g; Total Sugars: 24g; Protein: 5g

Strawberry Donut Bites

Servings: 6
Prep Time: 10 Minutes | Cooking Time: 25 Minutes
Ingredients:
- 2/3 cup flour
- A pinch of salt
- 1/2 tsp baking powder
- 1 tsp vanilla extract
- 2 tbsp light brown sugar
- 1 tbsp honey
- 1/2 cup diced strawberries
- 1 tbsp butter, melted
- 2 tbsp powdered sugar
- 2 tsp sour cream
- 1/4 cup crushed pretzels

Directions:
1. Preheat air fryer at 165°C/325°F.
2. In a bowl, sift flour, baking powder, and salt.
3. Add in vanilla, brown sugar, honey, 2 tbsp of water, butter, and strawberries and whisk until combined.
4. Form dough into balls. Place the balls on a lightly greased pizza pan, place them in the frying basket, and Air Fry for 10-12 minutes.
5. Let cool onto a cooling rack for 5 minutes.
6. Mix the powdered sugar and sour cream in a small bowl, 1 tsp of sour cream at a time until you reach your desired consistency.
7. Gently pour over the donut bites. Scatter with crushed pretzels and serve.
8. **Variations & Ingredients Tips:**
9. Use other fresh or frozen berries instead of strawberries.
10. Top with a cream cheese glaze.
11. Roll in cinnamon-sugar before baking.
12. **Per serving:** Calories: 135; Total Fat: 3g; Saturated Fat: 2g; Cholesterol: 10mg; Sodium: 105mg; Total Carbs: 25g; Dietary Fiber: 1g; Total Sugars: 10g; Protein: 2g

Hasselback Apple Crisp

Servings: 4
Prep Time: 15 Minutes | Cooking Time: 20 Minutes
Ingredients:
- 2 large Gala apples, peeled, cored and cut in half
- ¼ cup butter, melted
- ½ teaspoon ground cinnamon
- 2 tablespoons sugar
- Topping
- 3 tablespoons butter, melted
- 2 tablespoons brown sugar
- ¼ cup chopped pecans

- 2 tablespoons rolled oats*
- 1 tablespoon flour*
- vanilla ice cream
- caramel sauce

Directions:
1. Place the apples cut side down on a cutting board. Slicing from stem end to blossom end, make 8 to 10 slits down the apple halves but only slice three quarters of the way through the apple, not all the way through to the cutting board.
2. Preheat the air fryer to 165°C/330°F and pour a little water into the bottom of the air fryer drawer. (This will help prevent the grease that drips into the bottom drawer from burning and smoking.)
3. Transfer the apples to the air fryer basket, flat side down. Combine ¼ cup of melted butter, cinnamon and sugar in a small bowl. Brush this butter mixture onto the apples and air-fry at 165°C/330°F for 15 minutes. Baste the apples several times with the butter mixture during the cooking process.
4. While the apples are air-frying, make the filling. Combine 3 tablespoons of melted butter with the brown sugar, pecans, rolled oats and flour in a bowl. Stir with a fork until the mixture resembles small crumbles.
5. When the timer on the air fryer is up, spoon the topping down the center of the apples. Air-fry at 165°C/330°F for an additional 5 minutes.
6. Transfer the apples to a serving plate and serve with vanilla ice cream and caramel sauce.
7. **Variations & Ingredients Tips:**
8. Use Honeycrisp, Fuji, or Granny Smith apples for a tarter flavor.
9. Add dried cranberries or raisins to the topping mixture.
10. Drizzle with melted peanut butter or Nutella for extra decadence.
11. **Per Serving:** Calories: 370; Total Fat: 24g; Saturated Fat: 12g; Sodium: 150mg; Total Carbohydrates: 39g; Dietary Fiber: 4g; Total Sugars: 30g; Protein: 3g

Dark Chocolate Peanut Butter S'mores

Servings: 4
Prep Time: 5 Minutes | Cooking Time: 6 Minutes
Ingredients:
- 4 graham cracker sheets
- 4 marshmallows
- 4 teaspoons chunky peanut butter
- 113 grams dark chocolate
- ½ teaspoon ground cinnamon

Directions:
1. Preheat the air fryer to 200°C/390°F. Break the graham crackers in half so you have 8 pieces.
2. Place 4 pieces of graham cracker on the bottom of the air fryer. Top each with one of the marshmallows and bake for 6 or 7 minutes, or until the marshmallows have a golden brown center.
3. While cooking, slather each of the remaining graham crackers with 1 teaspoon peanut butter.
4. When baking completes, carefully remove each of the graham crackers, add 28 grams of dark chocolate on top of the marshmallow, and lightly sprinkle with cinnamon. Top with the remaining peanut butter graham cracker to make the sandwich.
5. Serve immediately.
6. **Variations & Ingredients Tips:**
7. Use milk chocolate or white chocolate instead of dark chocolate.
8. Substitute peanut butter with Nutella, almond butter, or cookie butter.
9. Add sliced bananas or strawberries for a fruity twist.
10. **Per Serving:** Calories: 320; Total Fat: 18g; Saturated Fat: 7g; Sodium: 180mg; Total Carbohydrates: 37g; Dietary Fiber: 3g; Total Sugars: 22g; Protein: 6g

Pecan-oat Filled Apples

Servings: 4
Prep Time: 10 Minutes | Cooking Time: 20 Minutes
Ingredients:
- 2 cored Granny Smith apples, halved
- 1/4 cup rolled oats
- 2 tbsp honey
- 1/2 tsp ground cinnamon
- 1/2 tsp ground ginger
- 2 tbsp chopped pecans
- A pinch of salt
- 1 tbsp olive oil

Directions:
1. Preheat air fryer to 190°C/380°F.
2. Combine together the oats, honey, cinnamon, ginger, pecans, salt, and olive oil in a bowl.
3. Scoop a quarter of the oat mixture onto the top of each half apple.
4. Put the apples in the frying basket and Roast for 12-15 minutes until the apples are fork-tender.
5. **Variations & Ingredients Tips:**
6. Use other types of apples like Honeycrisp or Fuji.
7. Substitute pecans with walnuts or almonds.
8. Drizzle with caramel sauce before serving.
9. **Per serving:** Calories: 160; Total Fat: 8g; Saturated Fat: 1g; Cholesterol: 0mg; Sodium: 50mg; Total Carbs: 22g; Dietary Fiber: 4g; Total Sugars: 14g; Protein: 2g

Peanut Butter-banana Roll-ups

Servings: 4

Prep Time: 10 Minutes | Cooking Time: 20 Minutes
Ingredients:
- 2 ripe bananas, halved crosswise
- 4 spring roll wrappers
- 1/4 cup molasses
- 1/4 cup peanut butter
- 1 tsp ground cinnamon
- 1 tsp lemon zest

Directions:
1. Preheat air fryer to 190°C/375°F.
2. Place the roll wrappers on a flat surface with one corner facing up.
3. Spread 1 tbsp of molasses on each, then 1 tbsp of peanut butter, and finally top with lemon zest and 1 banana half. Sprinkle with cinnamon all over.
4. For the wontons, fold the bottom over the banana, then fold the sides, and roll-up.
5. Place them seam-side down and Roast for 10 minutes until golden brown and crispy.
6. Serve warm.
7. **Variations & Ingredients Tips:**
8. Use other nut butters like almond or cashew butter.
9. Drizzle with honey before serving.
10. Roll in crushed graham crackers or granola after baking.
11. **Per serving:** Calories: 315; Total Fat: 12g; Saturated Fat: 2g; Cholesterol: 0mg; Sodium: 150mg; Total Carbs: 51g; Dietary Fiber: 4g; Total Sugars: 28g; Protein: 6g

Black And Blue Clafoutis

Servings: 2
Prep Time: 10 Minutes | Cooking Time: 15 Minutes
Ingredients:

- 15-cm pie pan
- 3 large eggs
- 1/2 cup sugar
- 1 teaspoon vanilla extract
- 2 tablespoons butter, melted
- 1 cup milk
- 1/2 cup all-purpose flour*
- 1 cup blackberries
- 1 cup blueberries
- 2 tablespoons confectioners' sugar

Directions:
1. Preheat the air fryer to 160°C/320°F.
2. Whisk eggs and sugar until smooth and lighter in color. Add vanilla, butter and milk.
3. Add flour and whisk just until no lumps remain.
4. Grease a 15-cm pie pan. Scatter half the berries in the pan.
5. Pour half the batter over berries and place in air fryer basket (use foil sling).
6. Air fry at 160°C/320°F for 15 minutes until puffed and slightly jiggly.
7. Remove, invert onto a plate and let cool while baking second batch.
8. Serve warm, dusted with confectioners' sugar.
9. **Variations & Ingredients Tips:**
10. Use any combination of fresh berries.
11. Drizzle with maple syrup or honey after baking.
12. Serve with whipped cream or vanilla ice cream.
13. **Per Serving:** Calories: 410; Total Fat: 13g; Saturated Fat: 6g; Sodium: 168mg; Total Carbohydrates: 68g; Dietary Fiber: 5g; Total Sugars: 42g; Protein: 9g

Vegan Brownie Bites

Servings: 10
Prep Time: 10 Minutes | Cooking Time: 8 Minutes
Ingredients:
- 2/3 cup walnuts
- 1/3 cup all-purpose flour
- 1/4 cup dark cocoa powder
- 1/3 cup cane sugar
- 1/4 teaspoon salt
- 2 tablespoons vegetable oil
- 1 teaspoon pure vanilla extract
- 1 tablespoon almond milk
- 1 tablespoon powdered sugar

Directions:
1. Preheat the air fryer to 175°C/350°F.
2. To a blender or food processor fitted with a metal blade, add the walnuts, flour, cocoa powder, sugar, and salt. Pulse until smooth, about 30 seconds.
3. Add in the oil, vanilla, and milk and pulse until a dough is formed.
4. Remove the dough and place in a bowl. Form into 10 equal-size bites.
5. Liberally spray the metal trivet in the air fryer basket with olive oil mist. Place the brownie bites into the basket and cook for 8 minutes, or until the outer edges begin to slightly crack.
6. Remove the basket from the air fryer and let cool. Sprinkle the brownie bites with powdered sugar and serve.
7. **Variations & Ingredients Tips:**
8. Use other nut varieties like pecans or almonds.
9. Add chocolate chips or dried fruit to the batter.
10. Use oat flour instead of regular flour to make gluten-free.
11. **Per** serving (1 brownie bite): Calories: 110; Total Fat: 7g; Saturated Fat: 1g; Sodium: 50mg; Total Carbs: 12g; Dietary Fiber: 2g; Total Sugars: 6g; Protein: 2g

INDEX

A

All-in-one Breakfast Toast 16

Artichoke-spinach Dip 25

Asian Glazed Meatballs 96

Beef & Spinach Sautée 47

B

Beer Battered Onion Rings 24

Black And Blue Clafoutis 106

Black Bean Veggie Burgers 91

Blistered Shishito Peppers 20

Blossom Bbq Pork Chops 41

British Fish & Chips 59

Buttered Brussels Sprouts 82

C

Caprese-style Sandwiches 73

Carne Asada 46

Cheddar & Egg Scramble 17

Cheesy Chicken-avocado Paninis 37

Chia Seed Banana Bread 15

Chicken Burgers With Blue Cheese Sauce 36

Chicken Gyros 87

Chicken Parmigiana 38

Chili Cheese Dogs 90

Citrusy Brussels Sprouts 77

Classic Crab Cakes 52

Classic Salisbury Steak Burgers 49

Colorful French Toast Sticks 13

Corn & Shrimp Boil 56

Corn Dog Muffins 23

Crabmeat-stuffed Flounder 54

Cream Cheese Deviled Eggs 10

Creole Tilapia With Garlic Mayo 61

D

Dark Chocolate Peanut Butter S'mores 104

Dijon Thyme Burgers 84

E

Eggplant Parmesan Subs 94

F

Fennel & Chicken Ratatouille 30

Feta & Shrimp Pita 58

Five-spice Roasted Sweet Potatoes 77

Fluffy Vegetable Strata 18

Fried Pickles 21

G

Green Peas With Mint 83

H

Hasselback Apple Crisp 102

Hot Cauliflower Bites 28

I

Inside Out Cheeseburgers 95

K

Korean-style Fried Calamari 60

L

Leftover Roast Beef Risotto 42

Light Frittata 14

M

Maple Bacon Wrapped Chicken Breasts 29

Meatless Kimchi Bowls 72

Mediterranean Salmon Cakes 57

O

Oatmeal Blackberry Crisp 100

Onion Rings 79

P

Patatas Bravas 78

Peanut Butter-banana Roll-ups 105

Pecan-oat Filled Apples 105

Perfect Burgers 89

Pesto Pepperoni Pizza Bread 70

Pigs In A Blanket 11

Provolone Stuffed Meatballs 86

R

Reuben Sandwiches 93

Rib Eye Cheesesteaks With Fried Onions 43

Rigatoni With Roasted Onions, Fennel, Spinach And Lemon Pepper Ricotta 71

Roasted Jalapeño Salsa Verde 22

Roasted Veggie Bowls 68

Rumaki 26

S

Satay Chicken Skewers 35

Simple Baked Potatoes With Dill Yogurt 76

Sirloin Steak Bites With Gravy 51

Smokehouse-style Beef Ribs 48

Smoky Chicken Fajita Bowl 34

Speedy Shrimp Paella 62

Spiced Roasted Pepitas 19

Spiced Shrimp Empanadas 53

Spicy Pearl Onion Dip 27

Spicy Sesame Tempeh Slaw With Peanut Dressing 63

Steak Fajitas 44

Steak Fries 81

Strawberry Donut Bites 101

Strawberry Donuts 98

Strawberry Pastry Rolls 99

Sunday Chicken Skewers 32

T

Tandoori Chicken Legs 33

Tandoori Paneer Naan Pizza 67

Tasty Brussels Sprouts With Guanciale 80

Thai Chicken Drumsticks 39

Thai Turkey Sausage Patties 9

Toasted Choco-nuts 75

Two-cheese Grilled Sandwiches 66

V

Vegan Brownie Bites 108

Veggie Burgers 69

Veggie Fried Rice 65

Venison Backstrap 45

Printed in Dunstable, United Kingdom